at

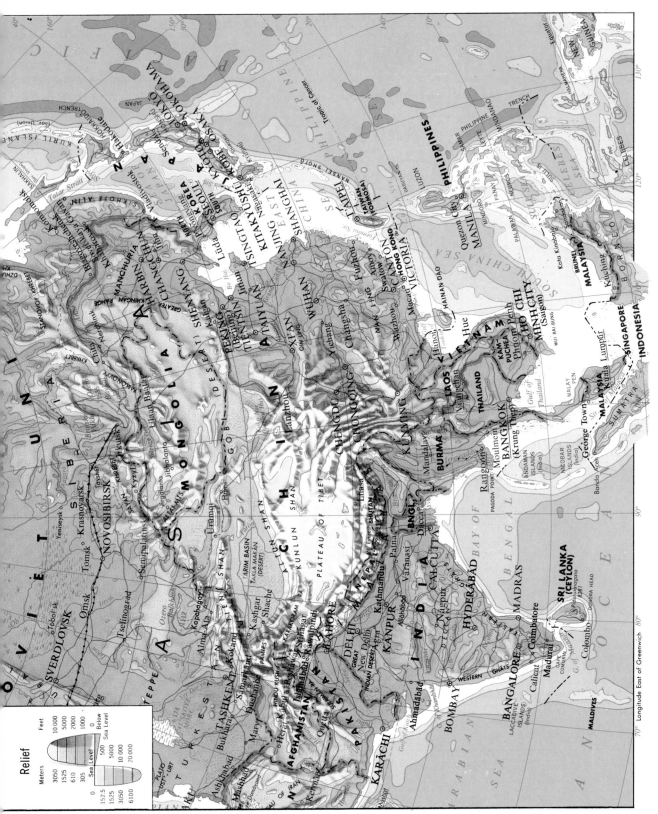

Enchantment of the World

PEOPLE'S REPUBLIC OF CHINA

By Valjean McLenighan

Consultants: Mikiso Hane, Ph.D., Szold Distinguished Service Professor of History, Knox College, Galesburg, Illinois

Lois Fusek, Ph.D., former Assistant Professor of Chinese Language and Literature, Department of Far Eastern Languages and Civilizations, University of Chicago

Stephen Burke, Undergraduate Asian Studies, University of Michigan, Ann Arbor

Consultant for Social Studies: Donald W. Nylin, Ph.D., Assistant Superintendent for Instruction, Aurora West Public Schools, Aurora, Illinois

Consultant for Reading: Robert L. Hillerich, Ph.D., Bowling Green State University, Bowling Green, Ohio

CHILDRENS PRESS™

CHICAGO

Songyue Pagoda, Chengchou (Zhengzhou)

Library of Congress Cataloging in Publication Data

McLenighan, Valjean.
  People's Republic of China.

  (Enchantment of the world)
  Includes index.
  Summary: An overview of China's history and life,
especially since, under the Chinese Communist party,
that country became the People's Republic of China
in 1949.
  1. China—History—1949-   —Juvenile literature.
[1. China] I. Title. II. Series.
DS777.55.M43 1984   951   84-7025
ISBN 0-516-02781-6   AACR2

Picture Acknowledgments

Annette Lerner, Colour Library International: Cover,
page 114 (top left)
Hillstrom Stock Photos: ©1984 Art Brown: Pages 4, 6
(top), 12, 24, 29, 32, 40, 44, 47 (left), 48, 49, 60, 61, 65, 68
(top), 72, 85 (right), 86 (bottom), 89, 93 (top), 95 (left), 97,
98, 99 (bottom right), 100 (bottom left and right), 102, 103,
104, 105 (left), 109, 113, 114 (top right), 129, 130, 131
©Eugene G. Schulz: Page 5
©Willie Moy: Pages 6 (bottom), 99 (middle), 108
©Jack Lund: Pages 27, 110
©Bonnie Czaskos: Pages 37, 106, 133
©Duke Marx: Page 59
©Judy F. Cohen: Pages 79, 88, 114 (bottom right), 121
Historical Pictures Service, Inc., Chicago: Pages 9, 71
**New China Pictures Co./Historical Pictures Service, Inc.,
Chicago:** Pages 47 (right), 80, 105 (right)
**Ontario Science Centre, Toronto/China: 7000 Years of
Discovery:** Pages 16, 30
Root Resources: ©Florence P. Turner, FPSA: Pages 19, 93
(bottom left and right)
©Jane Shepstone: Pages 54, 75, 86 (top)
©Grace H. Lanctot, FPSA: Pages 85 (left), 125
©Eastfoto: Pages 42, 53, 70
Nawrocki Stock Photo: ©Ruth Dunbar: Pages 58, 99 (top)
©Paul Beltz: Pages 94, 99 (bottom left), 122
©J. Moshman: Page 95 (right)
©James A. Cudney: Pages 100 (top), 114 (bottom left and
middle)
Wide World Photos: Page 68 (bottom)
Len Meents: Map on page 42
**Courtesy Flag Research Center, Winchester,
Massachusetts 01890:** Flag on back cover

Cover: Kweilin (Guilin)

Peking schoolchildren in colorful costumes

TABLE OF CONTENTS

Two-year-old P'u Yi sat on the great throne (below) in the Hall of Supreme Harmony (above) when he was installed as China's new emperor in 1908.

Chapter 1

FROM EMPEROR
TO CITIZEN

The Great Ceremony of the Enthronement fell on December 2, 1908, a very cold day in the Forbidden City. Two-year-old P'u Yi (Pu Yi), the adopted son of Emperor T'ung-chih, was being installed as China's new emperor. The little boy shivered atop the huge throne in the Hall of Supreme Harmony. Before him, one Chinese official after another bowed low to the ground, kowtowing to the new ruler in the ancient manner.

P'u Yi began to fuss and to shout that he wanted to go home. His father, kneeling beside the throne, tried to comfort the child. He urged him not to cry, and promised that soon it would be finished. In fact, within three years, P'u Yi's government was overthrown.

The revolution that toppled P'u Yi was supposed to change the way the Chinese had lived for more than two thousand years. Since 221 B.C. China had been ruled by emperors and a small class of scholar-officials known as mandarins. They lived in splendor, while the common people—hundreds of millions of peasant farmers and city workers—toiled in poverty. The Republic of

China, established in January, 1912, was supposed to be governed by a president, a constitution, and a parliament, not by an emperor.

P'u Yi gave up his right to rule, but kept his title and way of life. He and his court continued to live in a fabulous Forbidden City palace in the heart of Peking (Beijing).

Little P'u Yi grew up in the traditional way of emperors. When he wanted to walk in the garden, three servants ran ahead to warn people to get out of the way. The boy walked with servants on either side, in case he needed support. Behind them came servants holding up a huge silk canopy, and still more servants carrying umbrellas, changes of clothing, and a seat in case the young emperor needed to rest. They were followed by the imperial tea servants, who were followed by several servants carrying first-aid equipment.

It's no wonder that P'u Yi, growing up in such luxury, came to think he was the most important person in the universe. He had little contact with the real world. The only people he saw were members of his court and the hundreds of servants who waited on him hand and foot.

Court officials and P'u Yi's teachers encouraged him to believe that the new republic was only a passing phase of Chinese history. Someday, they said, the emperor would be restored to power.

In fact, warlords did restore P'u Yi to power briefly in the summer of 1917. But after a few days he was forced off the throne again. In 1931, the Japanese invaded northeast China and made P'u Yi the puppet ruler of the state of Manchukuo (Manchuria). So in 1934, P'u Yi gained the throne for the third time and earned the nickname "Yo-yo Emperor."

In 1937, Japan invaded the rest of China and conquered a third

When the Japanese conquered northeastern China, they made P'u Yi (seated) the puppet ruler of the state of Manchukuo.

of the country. During World War II, Japan fought on the side of Germany and Italy against the United States and its allies, which included the Soviet Union. P'u Yi went along wholeheartedly with the Japanese. He lived in luxury, while the people of northeastern China were forced to give food, money, and supplies to Japan.

By the end of the war, even P'u Yi realized that the Japanese were using him. But the "Yo-yo Emperor" could do nothing about it. He was terrified of the Japanese. But he was even more afraid of what might happen to him if Japan lost the war. How would he account to the Chinese people for his cooperation with their conquerors?

Japan surrendered to the Allied forces in August of 1945, and World War II ended. P'u Yi was captured by Russian troops and

9

flown to the Soviet Union. He was kept under house arrest for five years. Though P'u Yi was a prisoner, members of his family were permitted to act as his servants.

In China, Communist and Nationalist troops fought a bloody civil war. P'u Yi's fondest hope was never to see China again. But when the Communists won the Chinese civil war, the Russians, who were also Communists, put P'u Yi on a train back to his homeland.

P'u Yi was sure he was doomed. But instead of being tortured or killed, he and his family were taken to a Communist prison, or "reeducation camp."

The Communists told P'u Yi that they did not want to kill him. Instead, they wanted him to "study properly and remold" himself.

As part of his reform, P'u Yi was put to work in a factory, making pencil boxes. There he was to learn to respect his fellow workers, rid himself of his emperor's airs, and appreciate the value of hard work.

P'u Yi began to study communism. He read works by Karl Marx, V.I. Lenin, Mao Tse-tung (Mao Zedong), and other Communists. They wrote of a way of life exactly the opposite of the life P'u Yi had had. Communists want to get rid of ruling classes. They believe that everyone in a country should share the wealth. Communists think that workers, through their government, should own their country's resources and manage them for the benefit of all people.

How strange those ideas must have seemed to a man like P'u Yi. "For the past forty years I had never folded my own quilt, or made my own bed," P'u Yi wrote. "I had never even washed my own feet or tied my shoes." It took ten years in prison for him to accept communism and become a "new man" of China.

As part of P'u Yi's reeducation, the Communists asked him to write a book about his life. At first the former emperor was afraid to tell how he had worked with the Japanese. Instead, he wrote a paper that made him look like their victim. In long "study sessions," P'u Yi's fellow prisoners and jailers made him see that only by telling the truth could he remold himself. P'u Yi wrote a second, more accurate, version and his study group praised his great progress.

In December of 1959, P'u Yi was pardoned by the Supreme People's Court. He took a train to Peking. It was the first time P'u Yi had ever traveled with ordinary workers. The Forbidden City, where once he had lived in splendor, had been made into a public park.

P'u Yi received his voter's card in November, 1960. He wrote, "It seemed the most valuable thing I had ever had."

These were remarkable words from a man who once had owned the most precious treasures of China. The change from emperor to citizen was complete. Until his death in 1967, P'u Yi spent his days as an ordinary Chinese worker.

P'u Yi's dramatic change mirrors the changes that China has seen in the twentieth century. The move from ancient empire to modern People's Republic is still in progress. It directly touches the lives of one fifth of the people on our planet—the one billion people who live in the People's Republic. In the years since the new government was founded, China has been transformed from a poor, backward nation to a power the world must reckon with. The cost has been tremendous—not just in money, but in lives. China has a long way to go toward becoming a modern country. Its success or failure in meeting the challenges of tomorrow will, one way or another, affect us all.

West Lake, in Hangchou (Hangzhou), was created by a dike in order to protect the town from the waters of the Fuchun River and Hangchou Bay.

Chapter 2

IN THE BEGINNING

China has the longest continuous history of any nation on earth. Other civilizations developed earlier than China's, but none of them has lasted until today.

China's prehistory goes back some 600,000 years. Fossils that old have been dug up near Lan-t'ien. They belong to an apelike people who were among the first of our species to make tools.

Modern people—*homo sapiens*—appeared in China about fifty thousand years ago. Hunters and gatherers at first, by 4000 B.C. they discovered how to farm. In the area around the Great Bend of the Yellow River (Huang Ho), the Chinese changed from a Stone Age to a Bronze Age culture.

Metal tools replaced stone. Methods for farming and herding improved. Dams and irrigation canals were built to control flooding and provide water for the fields.

People lived in close-knit family groups in Neolithic, or Stone Age, times. Gradually these clans formed tribes and chose chiefs. Neighboring tribes joined forces against other tribes. Powerful ruling families, or dynasties, arose.

Legends say that China's first dynasty, the Hsia (Xia), was founded by a man named Yü. He was the last of the Five

Emperors who presided over China's Golden Age. Under these great rulers, it was said, the government of the world was perfect. The five set up the ceremonies of government and the sacrifices to be made to the gods, mountains, and streams. They taught the difference between right and wrong and showed the people the right way to behave.

By the end of the Hsia dynasty, fine smooth pottery was being made on potter's wheels, and bronze vessels began to appear. Silk culture had been invented, and weaving was well developed. People were building houses of timber and also making carriages and boats. The written language contained several thousand characters, or logographs.

THE CHINESE LANGUAGE

The earliest examples of Chinese writing we possess date from about 1300 B.C. The main features of the language have remained relatively unchanged down to our present time. In order to understand why Chinese developed the way it did, it is necessary to keep in mind three fundamental characteristics of the language. First, Chinese is essentially monosyllabic. This means that words are usually, though not always, one syllable in length. Second, the total number of pronounceable syllables is fairly limited. And third, the language is full of *homophones*. Homophones are words with the same pronunciation but with different meanings. "Bear" meaning an animal, and "bear" meaning to endure are examples of homophones in English. It would have been very difficult for the Chinese to adopt an alphabetic system of writing since so many words would look exactly alike. Instead, Chinese uses *logographs,* or characters. A logograph is a letter, character, or symbol used to represent an entire word. There are four basic categories of characters in Chinese:

1. *Simple Pictograms,* or characters that represent drawings of objects. For example,
     sun 日 (ancient form ☉)
     moon 月 (ancient form ☽)
     tree 木 (ancient form ✳)
2. *Simple Ideograms,* or characters that depict an idea or a concept pictorially. For example,
     one, two, and three 一 二 三

---

3. *Composite Ideograms,* or characters formed by the combination of two or more simple characters that "suggest" the meaning of the new character. For example,

rain 雨 + field 田 = thunder 雷

The first three categories account for only a small minority of all Chinese characters, but they are the characters used for the most common objects and concepts. The majority of Chinese characters belong to the fourth category.

4. *Composite Phonograms,* or characters that use one part, the *radical,* to indicate the meaning, and another part, the *phonetic,* to indicate the sound. For example, earth 土 is a character that also functions as a radical. When added to the phonetic character fang 方, the resulting word is neighborhood 坊, pronounced *fang.*

What the written character showed the eye, however, was not always clear to the ear when spoken. There gradually came into use a system of tones that helped to reduce, if not eliminate, the number of sound-alike words. Each syllable in Chinese is pronounced in a prescribed tone. Modern Chinese uses four tones. The level tone (—), the rising tone (‿), the low tone (⌄), and the falling tone (⌍). The tones help to differentiate one homophone from another, and the use of the proper tone is necessary for correct pronunciation. For example, *hū* means "to call out," *hú* means "a lake," *hŭ* means "a tiger," but *hù* means "a door." It is this use of tones that accounts for the musical quality of Chinese that is so apparent to Western ears.

One of the major problems facing the Chinese people as they attempt to modernize is the complexity of their language. It takes a much longer time to learn to read and write Chinese than it does to learn a language written with an alphabet. Typewriters require several hundred keys. The typesetting of books, magazines, and newspapers is a formidable job. And, too, the numerous different dialects often make spoken communication difficult. A primary task undertaken by the People's Republic of China when it came to power in 1949 was a program of language reform. There were three main objectives: to simplify the written characters; to popularize *putonghua* (Mandarin); and to develop a Chinese phonetic alphabet that had sound symbols for the characters. All of these reforms are now well underway, and there has been a widespread increase in literacy. Some two thousand simplified characters are presently in common use. About 70 percent of the population speaks *putonghua,* although they may speak their own dialect as well.

Over the years, many different romanization systems have been used to represent the sounds of the Chinese language, thus creating much confusion. A romanization system uses letters of the Roman alphabet to show the pronunciation of a foreign word.

The most widely favored system is the Wade-Giles system, developed around 1880. To help make the Chinese language easier for all Chinese people to learn, the p'in-yin (pinyin) system was developed. It was introduced in 1958 to help in the study of the written characters and to encourage greater use of *putonghua.* It also provides a unified system of spelling Chinese names in Western languages.

The Wade-Giles system is used for proper names throughout this book. The p'in-yin spelling is shown in parentheses the first time a name appears. As of January 1, 1979, the p'in-yin system has been declared the official romanization system of China. The foreign ministry and the government press agency have been instructed to adopt it in all its contacts with other countries. Since that time, more and more Western publications also have begun to use it.

This huge Shang dynasty bronze vessel is decorated with a human face.

THE SHANG DYNASTY:
THE BEGINNING OF CHINESE HISTORY

Sometime in the eighteenth century B.C., legends say, the Hsia were defeated by a neighboring tribe, the Shang. They took over the middle and lower regions of the Yellow River. The Shang dynasty marks the beginning of documented Chinese history. Some written records survive, as do tombs and other remains found in Anyang, once the Shang capital.

The simple people—that is, most Chinese—lived in Stone Age pit dwellings. Their floors were sunk a few feet below ground level, and they were topped with beehive-shaped roofs. Most people farmed the land. The growing use of bronze made better weapons and tools possible. Farming improved, as did pottery, weaving, and other crafts. The Shang dynasty is famous for the fabulous bronze vessels, plates, ornaments, and weapons its workers produced.

Wheeled carts and chariots became common in Shang times. All these developments led to the growth of trade and increased wealth. The Shang started to use cowrie shells as money.

The workers did not benefit much from their own labor, however. Instead, all surplus, or leftover, wealth belonged to the kings, warriors, and priests, who formed the ruling class.

These people lived in beautiful, walled cities. Their houses and palaces were built by workers and slaves. The rulers wore fine silk clothes and read books made of bamboo strips and wooden tablets. The Shang began to think of themselves as superior people. They considered any other tribes to be barbarians.

The dynasty lasted about five hundred years. During this time Shang armies fought many wars against neighboring tribes. For centuries they beat back the barbarians. But all those wars drained the country and put heavy burdens on the common people.

THE CHOU: CHINA'S LONGEST-LASTING DYNASTY

Finally, in the twelfth century B.C., the slaves revolted. Just about that time, the tribe of Chou (Zhou) attacked the Shang from west of the Great Bend. Many Shang slaves crossed over to the Chou, and the Shang dynasty collapsed. The Chou king burned the royal palace and started his own dynasty.

The Chou dynasty ruled China for the next nine centuries (1122-221 B.C.) — longer than any other dynasty in Chinese history. The original Chou were nomads who were less civilized than the people they had conquered. But as the centuries passed, the Chou took over many features of the Shang way of life, such as the Shang writing system and methods of farming and making bronze.

Early Chou kings passed out lands as fiefs, or private estates, to the royal princes. The princes sent taxes and gifts to the king's court. They promised to be loyal and send troops to protect the king when necessary. Every so often they took part in ceremonies that showed they recognized the Chou king as their rightful lord and ruler. As the "Son of Heaven," the Chou king was the top authority in the land. He answered only to Heaven.

Things stayed that way for several hundred years. But new tribes arose in the north and west and began to attack the Chou. Local princes raised their own armies. They stopped paying tribute to the Chou king and began to fight among themselves. This period of Chinese history (481-221 B.C.) is called the Warring States era. It ended when the prince of a state called Ch'in emerged as the most powerful of the warlords. He overthrew the Chou king and started his own dynasty.

THE CH'IN AND HAN DYNASTIES: CHINA BECOMES AN EMPIRE

The Ch'in (Qin) (221-206 B.C.) united the country under a central government for the first time. Emperor Shih Huang-ti got rid of the vassal states and divided China into provinces and counties. These were ruled by officials from the central government. They collected taxes, enforced the law strictly, and drafted peasants for the army and for public works.

The Ch'in built a road system to connect different parts of the empire. The walls put up by local princes to keep out barbarians from the north were joined into the Great Wall of China. Coins, weights, and measures were standardized, and the writing system was simplified.

THE GREAT WALL

The Great Wall of China can be seen from a spacecraft 200 miles (322 kilometers) above the earth. It stretches some 1,500 miles (2,400 kilometers) across northern China. It took 300,000 workers to build the wall. And the job lasted almost fourteen years. The wall is made of earth, brick, and stone. It tapers from about 25 feet (8 meters) in width at the base to 15 feet (5 meters) at the top. Watchtowers stand guard every 200 to 300 yards (183 to 274 meters). The parts of the Great Wall that exist today date from the Ming dynasty (A.D.1368-1644).

Yet the Ch'in emperor did everything he could to stamp out ideas he considered dangerous. He burned thousands of books. After one trial alone, he sent hundreds of scholars to be burned alive.

The peasants fared even worse. They died by the thousands building roads and canals, serving in the army, and slaving in the cities. In 206 B.C. they revolted. Fighting raged for four years, until a leader of peasant origins became the new emperor and founded his own dynasty, the Han.

The Ch'in dynasty lasted only fifteen years. But the system of government that the Ch'in set up survived for twenty centuries. The new Han dynasty used it. And with only few exceptions, so did every dynasty that followed the Han until A.D. 1911.

The Han dynasty, which succeeded the Ch'in, was founded by a man who came from the peasant class. His descendants ruled for more than four hundred years (202 B.C.-A.D. 221). Under Han rulers, the empire more than doubled in size. Many advances were made in mathematics, astronomy, science, the arts, history, writing, and other fields. Han emperors opened a trade route to the West. Caravans followed the Old Silk Roads from northwestern China to India, Persia, and the Mediterranean countries.

In the first century of Han rule, the teachings of Confucius and his followers became the official word of the state.

THE TEACHINGS OF CONFUCIUS

Confucius (551-479 B.C.) was a wandering scholar who lived during a period when China was in chaos. A teacher and philosopher, Confucius looked back to China's Golden Age to find out what had gone wrong and how China could return to the right path.

In the Golden Age, said Confucius, people acted in good faith and lived in harmony. The world was shared by all alike. Worthy and able people governed. The old, the young, and the sick were cared for. There were no thieves or rebels because everyone lived unselfishly and with respect for others. People practiced the Great Way.

But after emperors and dynasties arose, said Confucius, the Great Way was lost. People became greedy and selfish. Private families took over the world. They used goods and labor for selfish ends. Evil and plotting came about. Rulers raised armies against each other.

Confucius thought that everyone should understand his or her place in the world, and what others expect. Then peace and righteousness would reign. He saw society as a sort of giant family whose members had certain well-defined duties and rights with respect to one another.

Confucius taught a code of behavior that singled out five relationships for people to understand: between father and son, husband and wife, older and younger brother, friend and friend, and most important, ruler and ruled.

The emperor was both son and father—the Son of Heaven and father of his people. His duty as a good son was to make offerings and sacrifices to heaven and his ancestors. As the father of his people, he was to set an outstanding example. If he were good, wise, and dignified and performed the proper ceremonies, his people would behave likewise. But a dishonest, harsh, or wicked ruler could not expect loyalty from his ministers or his people.

Confucius's teachings, and ideas added by others, were collected in a group of books that included the *Analects*. From the Han dynasty onward, the only way to become a mandarin, or member of the ruling class, was to be an expert in Confucianism. The Han rulers introduced the practice of selecting government officials by giving a series of tests on Confucian ideas. Students studied and memorized Confucian texts for years to prepare for the grueling civil service tests. From Han times until the twentieth century, the best way to get ahead in China was to do well on these tests. The system of government by Confucian scholars, established by the Han, kept Confucianism at the heart of Chinese culture for nearly two thousand years.

A PATTERN APPEARS

The rise and fall of the Han established a pattern in Chinese history. The Han came to power on a wave of peasant revolt. The first emperors took steps to improve life for the common people. They cut taxes, eased harsh laws, and freed slaves. The Han built more waterworks and cleared more land for farming. The supply of grain and silk increased. So did the population.

But the Han, like the dynasties before them, faced mounting pressure from barbarians to the north and west. In this case, the enemy was the Huns. Long and costly wars against the Huns took their toll on the common people. With large numbers of peasants drafted into the army, farmland was not properly cared for. There was famine in times of flood and drought. The Han raised taxes to pay for the wars. Peasants who couldn't pay lost their land to government officials. Mandarins, among their many other privileges, did not have to pay taxes. So the peasants who managed to till their land were taxed even more heavily.

As the mandarins and court officials grew in power and wealth, they started to plot against each other. Sometimes they joined forces to plot against the emperor. The peasants formed secret societies to fight the landowners. The emperor sent armies to put down peasant rebellions. But the army generals began to get their own ideas about seizing power.

Descendants of the first Han emperors grew greedy. They stopped caring about the common people, even though they were the ones who did most of the work. Different groups fought at court, while the barbarians kept up their attacks.

All this led to the collapse of the Han in A.D. 221. For nearly four centuries afterward, chaos reigned in China. Sixteen different states would eventually compete for power. During this period a religion called Buddhism spread to China and began to gain many converts.

THE SUI AND T'ANG DYNASTIES

The Sui managed to unite the empire in 589, but they were overthrown thirty years later by the T'ang (Tang).

Under the T'ang (618-907), China became the largest country in the world. The empire stretched west through central Asia as far as the Pamir Mountains. It included Mongolia and Manchuria in the north. Tibet and Korea were vassal states. Chinese influence spread throughout Asia and was especially strong in Japan. Trade, art, and poetry flourished, and Buddhism in China reached its peak.

The T'ang rulers were content to leave society basically as it was. Early emperors took steps to make life easier for the peasants. They got rid of heavy taxes and forced labor. They divided the

*This Buddha is in
a Sian (Xian) temple.*

BUDDHISM

Buddhism came to China from India. Traders and missionaries carried the religion over caravan routes from the first to the third centuries A.D. The Chinese gave Indian Buddhism some new twists, which essentially created a new religion.

Buddhism teaches that life is suffering. It also preaches reincarnation—that is, when a person dies, the soul is reborn in a new body. A person's misery will be endless, say the Buddhists, until he learns to overcome his sense of self and rid himself of all earthly desires and attachments. This could take many lifetimes. The Buddhists' goal is to reach *nirvana*—free from the cycle of rebirth, in a state of heavenly peace and oneness with the universe.

There were seven schools of Buddhism in China. But the strongest and most purely Chinese was "Chan," or meditative, Buddhism. The complete absence of thought ("non-attachment") is achieved by sitting in meditation and getting back to the original, pure self.

By the sixth century A.D., Buddhism was widely accepted in China. The new religion coexisted with Confucianism and Taoism. Many Chinese considered these schools of thought as "three ways to one goal."

TAOISM

Taoism was a religion based on the *Tao*, or natural way to truth. Taoists disapproved of the elaborate ceremonies or ideas of government put forward by Confucius. They thought living simply, in harmony with nature, was the way to find peace. The truth of the Tao could not be explained in words alone. It had to be felt or experienced directly. Followers of this mystical religion tended to withdraw from public life. "Those who strive for nothing cannot be disappointed" was one favorite Taoist saying.

The Taoist symbol of yin and yang shows that harmony in the universe consists of a perfect balance between two great forces of nature. Yin, the dark part of the circle, stands for the female principle of life, as well as for the earth. Yang, the light part, represents the male life force, and the sky.

Legend has it that Lao-tzu (575-485? B.C.), the first great teacher of Taoism, lived about the same time as Confucius. Some people doubt that Lao-tzu ever existed. But the teachings of Taoism eventually were collected in the *Tao Te Ching (Daode Jing),* or *Classic of the Way and Virtue*. By the time the Han dynasty came to power, Taoism had a strong hold on Chinese life.

land more equally. But the T'ang relied on the mandarins, or scholar-officials, to govern. The mandarins did not have to pay taxes, join the army, or donate labor to the state. Power and wealth stayed in the same, educated hands. As the years went by, the mandarins began to control more and more land.

The same forces that toppled the Han led to the fall of the T'ang in 907. More than fifty years of civil war followed before the Sung reunited the country in 960.

THE SUNG DYNASTY AND THE GROWTH OF CITIES

The Sung (Song) (960-1280) cleared more land for farming and built massive water-control projects. The food supply increased, and the population doubled to 100 million by the end of the dynasty. Defeated by the northern barbarians, the Sung dynasty was forced to move its capital south of the Yangtze (Chang) River — the first time that the center of Chinese life moved from the Yellow River region. Instead of the caravan outposts along the Old Silk Roads, the coastal ports of east China became the main points of contact with the outside world.

There was another important shift under the Sung — from the country to the city. As the rural population grew, huge numbers of workers joined the shopkeepers, merchants, and artisans who jammed the cities. Hangchou (Hangzhou) alone had a population of two million. For the first time, the main source of government income shifted from the land to the cities. There was more money to be made taxing silk, tea, pottery, and other trade items than from taxing grain.

As the cities grew in importance, pottery, poetry, painting, and other art forms reached new heights. The Chinese began to print books by means of movable type. They invented the compass and the abacus. Gunpowder was discovered. But Sung society had its dark side, too. Poverty spread from the countryside to the cities. Never before had China seen so many urban poor. The government put some money aside to help them. But most of it ended up in the mandarins' pockets.

Women suffered greatly during the Sung times. For centuries the Chinese had believed the Confucian teaching that women were inferior to men. But women workers were vital in keeping farms going, and everyone knew it. In the cities, women's roles were not so clear-cut. Among the Sung mandarins, women became little more than playthings or signs of wealth.

The upper classes started to bind their little girls' feet so they grew to only half the normal length, with the toes turned under. In time, the painful practice became so widespread in China that a girl with normal feet was considered a freak.

The Sung dynasty rose and fell along the same lines as its predecessors. By this time, the pattern was well established in Chinese history. Early reforms did some good for the poor. But power and land became concentrated in the hands of the mandarins, who started to plot and fight among themselves. As the rich became greedier, the peasants formed secret societies to oppose them. Army leaders sent to put down peasant rebellions grew dangerous themselves. At court, different groups plotted against each other and the emperor. Later emperors were increasingly corrupt.

Meanwhile, as usual, the barbarians were pounding at the gates. Having conquered northern China, the Mongols swept down to occupy all of China by 1280. For the first time, China fell under barbarian rule.

This Chinese grandmother's feet were bound when she was a little girl. The practice, begun during Sung times, continued until the twentieth century.

THE YUAN (MONGOL) DYNASTY

Kublai Khan founded the Yuan dynasty (1280-1368). He was prince of a fierce tribe of nomadic warriors, the Mongols, whose empire included Russia and Persia as well as China. The Mongols knew nothing about farming or cities. Distrustful of the native Chinese, they relied on educated foreigners from other parts of the Mongol Empire to run the Chinese government.

One of these foreign officials was Marco Polo, a trader from Venice, Italy. He served Kublai Khan for nearly twenty years and wrote a book about his experiences in China. Though Polo's book was dismissed as fantasy by Europeans during his lifetime, it later played an important role in the spread of Chinese ideas and inventions during the fourteenth and fifteenth centuries.

The Mongols kept their own customs and language. But Kublai Khan also encouraged native Chinese arts, crafts, and learning. He built a beautiful capital at Peking. The fine pottery of the Sung dynasty was preserved, and high-quality silks and cottons were woven. The use of paper money spread, long before it was known in Europe. Kublai Khan introduced a new alphabet that could be used for any language in the empire. This period saw the emergence of the dramatic form as plays were written by scholars who could no longer hold public office.

By the middle of the fourteenth century, the Chinese Mongols had forgotten their old, warlike ways. Yuan rulers who came after Kublai Khan grew weak and corrupt. So much land had been seized from the peasants that one sixth of the native population was starving. Peasant uprisings began to occur. Finally, a former Buddhist monk fanned the sparks of discontent into a revolt that threw out the Yuan in 1368 and established the Ming dynasty.

Chu Yuan-chang (Zhu Yuanzhang), the first Ming emperor, was a former Buddhist monk.

THE MING DYNASTY: CHINA LOOKS TO ITS PAST

The Ming (1368-1644) restored the system of government by Confucian mandarins. They repaired the Great Wall and put the farms back in working order. Emperor Yung Lo (1360-1424) collected all of China's wisdom in one great encyclopedia.

Under Yung Lo, who reigned from 1403 to 1424, China built huge fleets and sailed to India, Arabia, and the east coast of Africa. But the voyages stopped after Yung Lo's death. The Ming dynasty was more interested in looking inward and backward to China's glorious past than in exploring the rest of the world.

Just the opposite was happening in Europe. A great age of sea exploration was beginning. By the end of the Ming dynasty, Portugal, Spain, Great Britain, France, and The Netherlands were all pressing China for trading opportunities. Japan, too, was prowling the coast.

This two-story silk draw loom is a reproduction of a Ch'ing (Qing) dynasty loom.

The fall of the Ming followed the usual pattern of Chinese history. Early reforms were undone by corruption and peasant abuse. Barbarian pressure added to tensions at home. Peasant uprisings became widespread. In the early 1630s, two rebel armies ravaged the land and overthrew the Ming dynasty. The rebels did not live to found a new dynasty, however. A barbarian tribe called the Manchus broke through the Great Wall and in 1644 established the Ch'ing dynasty.

THE CH'ING (MANCHU) DYNASTY: THE END OF THE IMPERIAL AGE

China prospered during the first 150 years of the long Manchu rule (1644-1911). The Manchus absorbed the Chinese way of life so easily that within a few generations very few spoke their native language. Still, they were despised as barbarians by the native Chinese.

The last hundred years of the Manchu dynasty were disastrous for China. The Ch'ing (Qing) faced the same problems that had toppled earlier ruling families—widespread rebellion at home and mounting pressure from foreign invaders. The rapid growth in population made poverty among the peasants worse than ever.

The Taiping Rebellion (1851-64) was the greatest civil war the world had ever seen. Millions died in the uprising. It was led by a Chinese Christian who preached the need for major changes in Chinese society, including treating women as equals of men.

The Boxer Rebellion of 1900, though not nearly so destructive, was better known in the West. It was directed against the Europeans in China, whose stranglehold had been tightening since the middle 1800s.

Forbidding mountains were among the geographical barriers that protected China from the rest of the world for most of its history.

For most of its history, China's geography protected it from the rest of the world. Forbidding deserts and mountains, plus a coastline on the widest stretch of the Pacific Ocean, provided a certain privacy. China traded goods and exchanged ideas along the Old Silk Roads and, later, by sea routes. Papermaking and movable type; silk culture, fine porcelains, and gunpowder; advances in medicine, mathematics, and science—these were among the developments that passed from China to the West. By comparison, the flow of ideas from Europe to China was light.

Since ancient times, the Chinese had thought of their country as the only real center of civilization. In fact, the Chinese name for their country, *Chung kuo (Zhongguo)*, means "Middle Kingdom" or "Central Kingdom." For centuries, the Chinese developed along

their own lines, confident in the belief that the rest of the world—
the barbarians—had little to offer.

The balance of trade supported this view until the early 1800s.
Barbarian demand for Chinese silk, tea, and porcelains was far
greater than China's imports of foreign goods.

But things changed during the nineteenth century. Europe,
America, and then Japan experienced the Industrial Revolution.
They began to develop heavy industry and capitalist economies.
While the Chinese had been content, for the most part, to stay in
their own part of the world, Westerners had fought and traded
their way into every corner of the globe. Their way of life
depended on finding ever-expanding markets for trade. And they
had the ships, soldiers, and modern weapons to impose their
point of view on people and nations that wanted nothing to do
with them.

These Europeans were different from any other barbarians the
Chinese had faced. But the Manchus woke up too late. After the
Opium War with Great Britain (1839-42), China was forced to
import opium from British India. Many ports were opened to
foreign merchants, and all trade was put under European control.

After losing a war with Japan (1894-95), China was forced to
give up Korea, Taiwan, and the Pescadores.

By the late nineteenth century, France, Great Britain, Germany,
Russia, and Japan had all rushed in to carve out "spheres of
influence" in China. A sphere of influence was an area where a
foreign power could build railways, naval bases, commercial
ports, or whatever else it wanted without competition from other
nations or interference from China. The Central Kingdom was
under the thumb of barbarians who actually considered the
Chinese an inferior race!

The Manchus were not only facing a new breed of barbarians. They also were facing a new breed of rebels. For the first time in Chinese history, the people revolted against the imperial system of government, not just against a particular dynasty.

NATIONALISM, DEMOCRACY, AND THE PEOPLE'S LIVELIHOOD

Many rebel groups were at work during the closing days of the Ch'ing. In 1905 Sun Yat-sen united these groups to bring down the Manchus.

Sun Yat-sen (1866-1925), a Christian, was the son of a Canton (Guangzhou) farmer. As a young man, he studied in Hawaii, Hong Kong, and London and became a physician. In the 1890s he formed a secret anti-Manchu society. By 1895 there was a price on his head in China, and he had to leave the country. He traveled to Japan, America, and England, trying to raise money and support for his one dream—to see China become a republic. To that end, he organized the Revolutionary League in 1905.

Sun's program consisted of the Three People's Principles: Nationalism, Democracy, and the People's Livelihood.

Nationalism meant that China should be free to run its own affairs without interference from foreigners. Democracy meant rule by a parliament and constitution. The People's Livelihood meant that the land and other resources should be managed for the benefit of the masses of people, not just to fatten the ruling classes.

Yuan Shih-k'ai (Yuan Shikai), the general of the imperial army, realized that the Manchus' days were numbered. Yuan made a deal with the rebels, and the boy emperor P'u Yi was forced to abdicate. Sun Yat-sen was sworn in as president of the new Republic of China on January 1, 1912. But his term lasted only forty-three days.

Yuan forced Sun to resign and made himself President for Life. He rewrote the constitution so that the post would pass to his son. The revolution had been double-crossed.

Yuan died in 1916, and warlords took over large sections of the country. To make matters worse, the Japanese were once again on Chinese soil.

Sun Yat-sen fell back and reorganized the Revolutionary League into the Kuomintang, or National People's Party (the Nationalists). Sun died of cancer in 1925, before he could see his Three People's Principles become a reality. But he is still honored today as the father of the Chinese Revolution.

Other reform-minded Chinese turned to the teachings of Marx, Lenin, and other Communists for answers to China's problems. They formed the Chinese Communist Party in 1921.

COMMUNISM

Karl Marx is often called the father of the Communist movement. He was a German philosopher, social scientist, and revolutionary who lived from 1818 to 1883. With the help of Friedrich Engels, another leading Communist thinker, Marx wrote the *Communist Manifesto* (1848), *Das Kapital* (1867), and many political articles that set forth Communist views.

Marx saw history as one long struggle between workers and the ruling classes who owned the land, factories, and other means of production. As long as these resources were privately owned, Marx wrote, the working classes were bound to suffer. Farm and factory profits would build up in the hands of the owners, and workers would have less and less share in the rewards of their labor.

Marx thought the free-enterprise system, or capitalism, was doomed. He admitted that it had produced great wealth in the highly industrial West. But a system that exploits the working classes is bound to collapse, said Marx. Capitalism had already led to widespread misery. When things got bad enough, the workers would revolt. They would seize the land, factories, and other means of production and run them for the common good. Everyone would share equally in the profits, and there would be no more conflicts between owners and workers, rich and poor. The march of history, said Marx, was toward public ownership of a community's resources, and toward society without classes.

Marx expected that communism would first take hold in a highly industrial country, such as England or Germany. In fact, the first successful Communist revolution occurred in Russia. The country was beginning to industrialize, but its wealth came chiefly from farming. V.I. Lenin and other Russian revolutionaries drew on Marx and Engels and added their own ideas. Lenin founded the Union of Soviet Socialist Republics in Russia in 1917. The writings of Lenin and Marx inspired Mao Tse-tung (Mao Zedong), Chou En-lai (Zhou Enlai), and other founders of the Chinese Communist Party.

COMMUNISTS AND NATIONALISTS UNITE

In 1923, Chinese Nationalists and Communists joined forces and set up a revolutionary government in Canton. They also established a military academy to train an army to send against

Chinese Nationalists and Communists joined forces in 1923 and set up a revolutionary government in Canton (Guangzhou) on the Pearl River (above).

the warlords. The dean of Whampoa Military Academy was Chiang Kai-shek, who became the leader of the Kuomintang, or Nationalists, after Sun Yat-sen's death in 1925.

Chiang feared that the Communists eventually wanted to take over the government. In fact, they secretly planned to do so when the time was right. But in 1926, each group needed the other.

A combined force of Communist and Nationalist soldiers, led by Chiang Kai-shek, left Canton in 1926 to march against the northern warlords. By March, 1927, they had taken Shanghai. But the following month, Chiang turned on the Communists. Thousands were shot down in the streets of Shanghai, and Communists were routed in other Kuomintang-controlled areas.

Early in 1928, Kuomintang forces reached Peking. The

Nationalist government controlled east-central China, the richest part of the country. Chiang set up his government in Nanking (Nanjing). America and other Western powers recognized it as the official government of China and sent aid.

CIVIL WAR

Warlords still controlled large areas in the north, west, and south. The Communists who survived Chiang's sudden attack holed up in the rugged mountains of Kiangsi (Jiangxi) Province in southeastern China. There they began to organize the peasants. At the end of 1931, the Communists proclaimed a Chinese Soviet Republic in Kiangsi.

In areas controlled by the Chinese Soviet Republic, with Mao Tse-tung as chairman, landlords and officials were driven out or killed. Their lands were given to the peasants, who elected their own councils, or *soviets.* Other much-needed reforms were carried out. By 1933, Communists numbered 300,000.

Japan invaded Manchuria in 1931. But instead of fighting the Japanese, Chiang Kai-shek concentrated on rooting out the Communists. In October, 1934, the main force of the Communist Red Army was holed up in southern Kiangsi, blockaded by Chiang's Nationalist forces. Led by Mao Tse-tung and General Chu Teh (Zhu De), more than a hundred thousand Communists broke through the blockade and traveled, on foot, some 6,000 miles (9,700 kilometers) to Shensi (Shaanxi) Province in the north. Only about twenty thousand survived the agonizing, yearlong journey that came to be known as the Long March. But along the way, the "Poor People's Army" won the support of millions of peasants.

For the next ten years, China was caught in a triangular war—between the invading Japanese on one hand, and the battling Nationalists and Communists on the other. For a brief time in the late 1930s, the Nationalists and Communists joined in an uneasy alliance against the Japanese. Japan surrendered to the Western Allies in August of 1945, and World War II ended. But civil war in China resumed.

Less than five years later, Communist forces had driven Chiang Kai-shek and what remained of his Nationalist troops to the island of Taiwan, off the eastern coast. There Chiang reestablished the Republic of China. The United States continued to recognize it as the only official government of China until 1979.

MAO TSE-TUNG

Mao Tse-tung (Mao Zedong) was the founder of the People's Republic of China and chairman of the Chinese Communist Party from 1935 to 1976. Born to a middle-class peasant family in Hunan Province in 1893, Mao studied history and the classics in a local school. He ran away from home in 1911 to Changsha, the provincial capital. There he studied, wrote, and met people with new political ideas. In 1918 he went to Peking and worked at the university library. He read the works of Karl Marx and helped to found the Chinese Communist Party in Shanghai in 1921.

In the early 1920s Mao began to see the role that peasants could play in bringing about a Communist revolution. He returned to his home province and in 1927 wrote a famous article, "Report on the Peasant Movement in Hunan."

Mao emerged in the early 1930s as an important figure. He won control of the party during the Long March (1934). In the late

Mao Tse-tung (Mao Zedong) in 1927

1930s and early 1940s he wrote many papers on politics, culture, and military affairs. These formed the basis of his future government. He led the Communist revolution to victory and on October 1, 1949, announced the founding of the People's Republic.

Chiang Kai-shek had begun his campaign against the Communists with a four-to-one edge in troops and weapons, and with massive support from the West. But the Nationalists failed to deal successfully with the staggering problems that faced China.

When the Nationalists took over, the country was still suffering from decades of civil war and exploitation by foreign nations. The poor people, as usual, were overworked, overtaxed, underpaid, and underfed. Chiang's government was not very successful at helping the peasants. Many Nationalist officials were greedy and corrupt. They made fortunes in the war while millions of Chinese citizens starved and suffered. Most of the government's resources continued to go to the military, not to the people.

The Communists, though they had far less to work with, offered hope to the Chinese people. In areas under their control, land reform was carried out. Where possible, the Communists set up schools and offered medical care. The force of the peasants, said Mao Tse-tung, was "like the raging winds and driving rain." And it was that force that finally drove him to victory.

Chapter 3

THE LAND AND ITS USES

The People's Republic of China, the third largest country in the world, dominates southern Asia. Only the Soviet Union and Canada exceed China in size. China's frontiers are among the longest in the world. It has borders with a dozen different countries. These include the Soviet Union and Mongolia in the north; Pakistan, Afghanistan, and India in the west; and Burma, Laos, and Vietnam in the south. About 3,600 miles (nearly 5,800 kilometers) of seacoast form the eastern boundary of the People's Republic. The coast stretches from Vietnam in the south to Korea in the north.

The territories at the top of the map of China lie as far north as Labrador in northeastern Canada. The city of Canton, on the other hand, is as far south as Cuba. Vast deserts, gently rolling farms, tropical jungles—China has all these features and more.

Lofty mountain ranges and high, dry plateaus cover much of the lonely, western two thirds of the People's Republic. A north-south mountain chain divides this area from eastern China.

Ninety percent of the Chinese people live in eastern China. This part of the country contains most of China's farms and industry. Though the west is developing rapidly, the eastern third of the

These farmers are sunning grain in northeastern China, the country's largest and most fertile farming area.

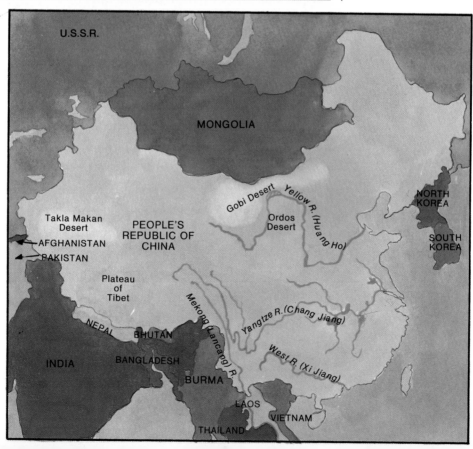

country is China's heartland. Roughly, it divides into four main areas: the northeast, and the three regions drained by China's major rivers as they flow to the coast from the high country—the Yellow (Huang Ho), the Yangtze (Chang), and the West (Xi).

NORTHEASTERN CHINA

Northeastern China is known as Manchuria to Westerners. The Japanese called it Manchukuo when they occupied it in the days before World War II.

The northeast provides much of China's food and industrial wealth. In the center of the region, farms grow sugar beets, soybeans, and wheat. This is China's largest and most fertile farming area—140,000 square miles (362,599 square kilometers) of gently rolling plains.

Coal and iron for the region's industries come from the Changpai Mountains in the east. The area produces about a third of China's coal, steel, and machine tools. The Russians and Japanese began building railroads and factories in the northeast at the turn of the century. Today, dams on the Yalu River provide electric power for North Korea and the People's Republic, while oil from the rich Taching fields fuels the economy.

Shenyang (Mukden), with a population exceeding 2.5 million, and Haerh-pin (Harbin) are two important cities in the region.

THE YELLOW RIVER REGION

The Yellow River (Huang Ho) begins in the western mountains and cuts through deep gorges before reaching the coast. The area it drains is the cradle of Chinese civilization. Some of China's

Cave dwellings in Honan Province

oldest prehistoric sites have been discovered around the Great Bend in the north. From there, Chinese culture spread south to the Yangtze River and beyond. The earliest of China's great ruling families built their capitals in the Yellow River region. Peking, the capital of the modern People's Republic, dates back to the thirteenth century. Tientsin (Tianjin) was one of China's earliest manufacturing cities.

The Yellow River takes its name from its color. The waters are muddied by fine particles of silt, called loess, carried by the winds from the northwest. In the provinces of Kansu (Gansu), Honan (Henan), Shansi (Shanxi), and Shensi (Shaanxi), millions of peasants live in hillside caves carved out of loess deposited over thousands of years.

The Yellow River is often called "China's Sorrow." Silt washed down from the high country gradually fills up the riverbed. For centuries, peasants have built and rebuilt dikes along the banks. Still, the river floods frequently. History records at least six floods severe enough to change the river's course.

Major floods destroy tens of thousands of square miles of farms and homes. They have killed millions of peasants in this region during the course of Chinese history. Yet the periodic flooding along the Yellow River has at least one benefit. As the waters pull back, they leave behind a rich layer of silt to fertilize the plains. Wheat and cotton grow in the region and poultry, pigs, and dairy cows are raised. Silk is a major industry in Shantung (Shandong) Province, while fishing is important in the delta.

THE YANGTZE RIVER REGION

The Chinese words for the Yangtze River (Chang Jiang) mean "long river." At 3,988 miles (6,418 kilometers), the Yangtze is the fifth longest river in the world. Unlike the Yellow River, which is useless for navigation, boats can travel more than 600 miles (966 kilometers) upstream from the mouth of the Yangtze. But shallows and rapids make it one of the world's most treacherous rivers.

The Yangtze doesn't flood as often as the Yellow River. But when it does overflow, terrible destruction can result. One of the worst floods occurred in 1931. Directly or indirectly, it killed more than 3 million people.

Several important cities lie along the Yangtze. China's most famous seaport, Shanghai, lies near the mouth of the river. About half of all Chinese exports pass through Shanghai. In the mid-1800s, Shanghai was the center of the opium trade in China. It had a worldwide reputation as a city of vice and violence. The Chinese Communist Party was founded there in 1921. After the revolution, the Communists succeeded in reducing the vice trade.

About 200 miles (322 kilometers) upstream lies Nanking. It served as the rebel capital in the most destructive civil war in history—the Taiping Rebellion of the mid-1800s. Later, Chiang Kai-shek made it his Nationalist government capital, but it was captured and sacked by the Japanese in 1937.

The city is an important industrial center for chemicals, machine tools, textiles, iron, steel, and cement. The surrounding area produces rice, wheat, millet, cotton, tea, and fruit.

Farther up the Yangtze is Wuhan, the collective name for the three industrial cities of Hankou, Hanyang, and Wuchang. The spark that touched off the 1911 revolution was ignited in Wuhan. Fifty years later, the area became an important center of activity in another great upheaval—the Cultural Revolution.

Several hundred miles upriver lies Chungking (Chongqing), a shipping and trading center for food grown in the Red Basin to the north. Rice, wheat, sugarcane, and cotton are harvested in the eleven-month growing season. The terraced hillsides produce tea, citrus trees, and the mulberry trees that are the heart of China's silk industry.

SILK

Chinese legends say that Empress Hsi Ling-shi discovered silk and invented a way to spin it around 2700 B.C. Whether the story is true or not, the art of silk making was a Chinese secret until about A.D. 550, when two monks smuggled silkworm eggs out of China and took them to Constantinople.

Most silk sold today is spun by silkworms raised by farmers. China is the world's second ranking raw-silk producer.

Female silk moths lay from three hundred to five hundred eggs each. The eggs hatch into tiny silkworms that eat fresh mulberry leaves continuously for four to five weeks. Then the worms are ready to spin their cocoons. During a three-day period, each worm spins a long single thread around itself. Farmers place the cocoons in hot ovens to kill the insects before they burst the thread.

The cocoons are soaked in hot water. Threads from several cocoons are wound together to form a single, strong fiber. Then the silk is boiled in hot soap to remove a sticky natural substance called sericin. The silk can be dyed before or after it is woven into cloth.

Rice (left) and tea (right), two of China's most important crops, grow in the semitropical southern regions of the country.

In all, the Yangtze drains an area of some 435,000 square miles (1,126,646 square kilometers). The region is densely populated. In fact, it contains more people than the Soviet Union and the rest of the Communist world combined. Szechwan (Sichuan) Province alone has more than 50 million people.

THE WEST RIVER REGION

Southern China, the area drained by the West River (Xi Jiang), is the poorest of the heartland's four main regions. It has long been known as a center for new ideas. Sun Yat-sen, who led the revolt that founded the Republic of China in 1912, came from the region's most important city, Canton. Other important leaders, including Chiang Kai-shek, Mao Tse-tung, and Chou En-lai, worked there during the twenties.

Rice, sweet potatoes, and tea grow in the semitropical southern regions. Kwangtung (Guangdong) Province is densely populated, especially in the Pearl River (Zhu Jiang) delta. There two or three rice crops can be harvested each year. But so little of the land is

Canton, in Kwangtung Province, is the most important city in the West River region.

suitable for farming that for centuries there was more emigration from Fukien (Fujian) and Kwangtung provinces than from any other part of Asia. Southern Chinese people emigrated to Taiwan, the Philippines, Southeast Asia, and the Americas. The area's reputation for restlessness and openness to new ideas is in part due to letters and visits home by "overseas" Chinese.

CLIMATE

Northeastern China has a cold, dry climate. Each of the three river basins of eastern China has a distinct climate. The Yellow River area is dry. Winters are hard and cold, and the slight rainfall is limited to summer months. The Yangtze Basin has a soft, wet climate. It is hot and humid in summer and cold and wet in winter. The West River area has a subtropical climate. Summers are hot and damp, and winters warm and sunny.

Between the Yellow River and the Yangtze, the Huai River divides eastern China in two. The north, a region of dry farming,

Wheat is one of the main crops of the dry farming region in the north of China.

produces millet, wheat, and maize as main crops. Forests are rare in northern China. In winter the land is brown and dusty. The growing season is four to six months long, and rainfall is limited to 15 to 25 inches (38 to 64 centimeters) yearly. Rains fall in the right quantities only every three or four years. Flood or drought is the rule. Since earliest times, northern China has depended on large-scale water-control projects to grow crops.

In southern China, on the other hand, the landscape is green all year round. Rain falls dependably, from 40 to 80 inches (102 to 203 centimeters) a year. The growing season lasts from nine to twelve months, and water is available for irrigation. In southern China, rice is the main crop. Farmers also plant tobacco, sweet potatoes, barley, and other foods.

THE WILD CHINESE WEST

Western China is a forbidding, lonely region, a lot like the American frontier of the old Wild West days. Snowcapped mountains stand like frozen sentries over high, dry valleys.

The Himalaya Mountains in the southwest anchor the cold, dry uplands of the Tibetan Plateau. The northern edge of the plateau is ringed by the K'unlun Mountains (Kunlun Shan). In the west, the Pamirs and the T'ien Mountains (Tien Shan) divide China from southern Russia. The Altai Mountains (Qilian Shan) run along the northern border.

Three great deserts—the Takla Makan, Gobi, and Ordos—form a chain sweeping eastward from the Pamir Mountains.

The vast Chinese frontier is rich in untapped natural resources. The northwest holds huge oil reserves. Gold, platinum, and uranium have been found in the frontier, as have massive deposits of coal and iron.

Much of the region is too high and dry for farming. But Sinkiang (Xinjiang) and Tsinghai (Qinghai) are two key areas in the government's plan to increase farmland. There huge waterworks have been built to reclaim the dry grasslands. Each year hundreds of thousands of Chinese workers migrate to the west.

The natives of the frontier, known as national minorities, face some of the same problems as Native Americans. Their customs, beliefs, and life-styles are different from the majority of Chinese— the Han. The national minorities number about 55 million in a total population of about 1 billion. Their way of life is sure to change as more and more Han Chinese move into their territory.

Industry in the west has expanded rapidly in recent times. In Kansu Province, a sprawling refinery processes oil from the western fields. Iron and steel plants dot the railroad line that connects the region to the east. Throughout the frontier, armies of workers mine deposits of coal, iron, lead, sulfur, and gold. It is here that China is testing its nuclear weapons.

Chapter 4

THE EARLY DAYS OF THE PEOPLE'S REPUBLIC

The Communists had their work cut out for them in the early days of the People's Republic. Their country lay close to ruins after decades of armed struggle. Transportation and communication networks had to be restored; farming had to be reorganized. The Communists were determined to transform China into a great industrial nation that would take its place proudly in the modern world. They also wanted to build a true Communist, or classless, society, in which all shared equally in the nation's wealth. The revolution affected every aspect of Chinese existence—agriculture, government, education, culture, even family life.

In the countryside and in the cities, supporters of the Nationalists were hunted down. At mass trials of so-called criminals and members of the landlord class, workers and peasants acted as judges and juries. In the early days of this period, which came to be called the Reign of Terror, former government officials, merchants, landlords, and Nationalist army officers often were beaten to death on the spot by their outraged victims. Others died in mass public executions or in "reform-through-labor" camps. No one knows how many hundreds of thousands—or perhaps millions—died in this first wave of revolutionary fury.

Later, efforts were made to reeducate skilled workers, technicians, and others with talents needed to build the new society. The idea was to change the thinking of non-Communists, and even of Communists who had strayed from the official party line. Relatives, friends, and fellow workers put pressure on people with "incorrect" thoughts to remold their thinking. Such people confessed their errors publicly and admitted that they had been "enemies of the people."

A FRIENDSHIP PACT—AND WAR

In the winter of 1949-50, Mao Tse-tung spent two months in Moscow. There he talked with Joseph Stalin, the leader of the Soviet Union, the world's other major Communist power. The Sino-Soviet Friendship Pact of February, 1950, provided a modest loan to China to help rebuild its economy. Russian specialists and equipment poured into China, and work began on restoring lines of transportation and communication. The two leaders also signed a military defense pact. Mao feared that anti-Communist governments, particularly the United States, would try to undermine his revolution.

In June, 1950, war broke out in Korea. The country had been annexed by Japan in 1910. But after World War II, Soviet troops took over the area north of the thirty-eighth parallel of latitude. American troops occupied the south. In late 1948, Korea held elections. A Communist government came to power in the north,

Units of the Korean People's Army and the Chinese People's Volunteers celebrate a victory over opposition United Nations troops during the Korean War in 1953.

and Soviet troops pulled out. The South Koreans elected a government that had the support of the United States.

North Korean troops invaded the south in June, 1950. Within days, United Nations troops, including American forces, came to South Korea's defense. They fought as far north as the Yalu River, which separates Korea from China.

Mao was outraged that the United Nations troops were so close to Manchuria. That region's industry and agriculture were vital to Mao's plans for rebuilding China. In the fall of 1950, Mao ordered Chinese troops into Korea. The bloody conflict seesawed back and forth until 1953, when an armistice divided Korea along almost the same line that had existed before the war.

In farm communes and cooperatives, established after the Communist takeover, Chinese peasants pooled their labor.

EARLY LAND REFORMS

While Chinese troops fought in Korea, Communists at home carried out the first stage of the land-reform movement. Even before the declaration of the People's Republic, farms in areas under Communist control had been given back to the peasants. Private households farmed individual plots with primitive methods and tools. Though they were freed from the control of the landowners, the peasants were still at the mercy of poor weather or bad luck. If someone in a household became ill, the harvest might suffer. Too much or too little rain could wipe out a family's entire income.

After the Communist takeover, peasants were urged to form mutual-aid teams of thirty to forty families. By pooling land and labor and working on each other's plots, they could raise larger crops in good times and avoid disaster in times of drought or flood. During busy times, such as planting and harvesting, more people shared the work. In slack periods, they cleared new fields for planting.

Such teamwork led to the establishment of cooperative farms. Income was shared among the members according to the amount of work each contributed.

Management of the farms was in the hands of the workers. Poor people who had never before managed anything more than a small plot of land were elected to positions of authority. They gained a new self-respect. The movement toward cooperative farming also increased the farmers' desire to learn to read and write.

THE FIRST FIVE-YEAR PLAN

It was important that the farms be productive. But another major goal of the government was to turn China into a great industrial power. In a Communist country, the central government plans and directs an overall program for the economy. The first Five-Year Plan was announced in 1953. As a result of this crash program, iron and steel output tripled by 1957, and coal production rose dramatically. With the help of loans from the Soviet Union, railroads, power plants, and dams were built.

More than half the existing factories and plants in the country were brought under state control. The government appointed the managers, who in some cases were the former owners. Factory owners who had not allied themselves with the Nationalists and were willing to work with the Communists received interest on their business investments. About a million of these "national capitalists" went to work for the revolution.

THE HUNDRED FLOWERS CAMPAIGN

In the early days of the People's Republic, newspapers, radio stations, books, and other communication media were placed under strict Communist Party control. Meetings without official approval were forbidden. In May, 1956, Chairman Mao decided to relax censorship and encourage criticism of "improper work style." The official party slogan was, "Let a hundred flowers bloom, let a hundred schools of thought contend."

At first, people were reluctant to talk, perhaps remembering the Reign of Terror. But with coaxing from high officials, discussions began. Students, teachers, writers, and even army officers talked openly about what they thought was wrong in the new China.

By the spring of 1957, a storm of protest had spread from Peking throughout the country. One newspaper reporter, a Communist for thirteen years, charged that party members made up a new priviliged class in China. They ate meat, he said, while ordinary workers and peasants went without. He even charged that Chairman Mao may have "committed errors."

Peasants and workers in Canton grew restless. There were riots in Wuhan. Clearly, the Hundred Flowers campaign had backfired. The party once again clamped down on the press. High officials who had spoken too freely were dismissed from office and made to publicly confess to crimes against the people. Hundreds of thousands of dissenters were sent off to labor camps.

THE GREAT LEAP FORWARD

In this "Rectification Campaign," people who spoke out for slow and careful development of China's industry and agriculture were silenced. The second Five-Year Plan, which came to be known as the Great Leap Forward, called for speedy and enormous increases in farming and industry.

The hard work of the Chinese people—plus favorable weather conditions—had made a success of the first Five-Year Plan. Government planners were so delighted that they seriously overestimated what could be accomplished in the second five years. The Great Leap Forward, announced in late 1957, called for doubling production targets in 1958. About 65 percent of the money budgeted for investment went to heavy industry. The collective farms were reorganized into giant People's Communes. But for a number of reasons, the Great Leap Forward failed to meet its goals.

In a little over a year, about 500 million workers were organized into 25,000 communes. In the early stages of the land-reform movements, there was still some private ownership of land, animals, and equipment. But under the new system, everything was owned by the commune, which operated under the central management of party officials.

In the typical commune, about 10,000 acres (4,047 hectares) of land were farmed by about five thousand households. The idea was to combine labor, machines, land, and capital to achieve the benefits of large-scale farming. With an entire district united as one giant farm, modern work methods could be used, and extensive land improvements could begin.

China's leaders hoped that farming would be efficient under this system. But things didn't work out as planned.

Some of the farmers resented giving up their land and being told what to plant and how and where to plant it. In their zeal to increase production, party officials tended to interfere too much.

Among the many natural disasters that China suffered during the years between 1959 and 1961 were floods. These flood markers on the Yangtze River show the various levels reached by the river's waters during periodic floods.

Many managers, as well as farmers, knew nothing about large-scale farming. All too often, they also lacked the equipment needed to succeed.

On top of these problems, China suffered a number of natural disasters in the years between 1959 and 1961. The north endured long periods of drought. In the south there were floods. Swarms of locusts devoured entire crops in some areas.

By 1961, food shortages were so severe that the government had to import millions of dollars' worth of grain to ward off mass starvation. It was clear that the Great Leap Forward had failed to improve agriculture. Very large communes proved difficult to manage, and smaller units soon became the norm.

Industrial production, too, was disappointing. Factory managers in a hurry to meet their targets put up with waste and sloppy workmanship. The government encouraged citizens to build

This cement-block factory may have developed from one of the backyard industries that were encouraged by the government in the early 1960s.

backyard furnaces near their homes for turning out crude iron. But this program failed, too. The homemade iron was of such low quality that it was practically worthless.

After 1962, the government announced a policy of "walking on two legs." Industry and agriculture would be developed simultaneously. The policy also called for a balance between heavy and light industry, large and small businesses, modern and ancient methods of production, and between programs run by the central government and those managed by local authorities.

The communes were encouraged to be independent as far as simple industrial products were concerned. They made their own common utensils, as well as bricks and other building materials. Commune workshops that had begun as repair centers started making tools. Some developed into small-scale industries. In these workshops many people acquired the skills needed for further industrial growth.

A commune middle school in Shensi (Shaanxi) Province

The communes became self-reliant units of both agricultural and industrial production. They marketed and distributed their own products locally and ran their own schools, health care, and other social services. They also became a basic unit of local government in China's Communist society.

CRACKS IN COMMUNIST UNITY

The failure of the Great Leap Forward caused bitter disagreement among the Chinese leadership. For the first time, cracks in party unity began to appear. Although Mao Tse-tung still wielded great authority, the post of chairman of the People's Republic passed to Liu Shao-ch'i (Liu Shaoqi) in April of 1959. Mao retained his position of chairman of the Communist Party.

Born in Hunan Province in 1898, Liu began his career as a labor organizer. He was elected to the Politburo, the Communists' government body, in 1932.

Agricultural communes, self-reliant units of production, marketed their own products locally. This farmer was selling pigs at a village market.

An aide to Mao Tse-tung, Liu completed the Long March. He became one of the leading thinkers in Chinese Communist circles. Liu's most famous work, "On How to be a Good Communist," appeared in 1939. When Mao went to Moscow in 1949-50, he left Liu in charge of affairs at home.

Liu was one of the first to suggest that China, not Russia, should lead the Third World revolutionary movement. Throughout the 1950s, Liu rose in party ranks. From 1959, when Liu replaced Mao as chairman of the People's Republic, until 1968, Liu played an active and important role in Chinese affairs.

After Liu came to power, border clashes with India were followed by a marked cooling in the relationship between the Soviet Union and China. A split had been growing for some time. Since the 1940s, certain Chinese Communists had resented what they considered Russia's lack of faith in their revolution—and lack of support for their fight against Chiang Kai-shek. True, the Soviet Union supplied economic aid to the new nation. But Russia's support was hardly massive, and it took the form of repayable loans, not outright grants.

The two nations had different ideas about what direction the world Communist movement should take. For the first time since the Russian Revolution of 1917, Soviet leadership of world communism was challenged.

Relations were strained further after Joseph Stalin's death in 1953. Nikita Khrushchev came to power in Russia. He denounced Stalin and publicly warned against the dangers of nuclear war. In a meeting with American political leader Hubert Humphrey in December, 1958, Khrushchev went so far as to praise President Dwight Eisenhower and declare, "We want no evil to the United States." Furthermore, he criticized China's People's Communes as "old-fashioned" and "reactionary."

The Chinese were angry. To them, the United States was communism's number one enemy. They felt Khrushchev had betrayed world communism. And his criticism of the People's Communes was a direct insult to China.

In June, 1959, Khrushchev canceled an agreement to supply the People's Republic with materials for nuclear weapons. He also stopped all economic aid. In 1962, the conflict between China and India erupted into a brief war. Russia expressed "regret" over the fighting and honored agreements to supply India with planes. The last straw came in 1963, when Russia signed a limited nuclear test ban treaty with Great Britain and the United States. The next year, China exploded its first nuclear device—without Soviet assistance. By then, the two nations were expressing their hostilities openly.

Chapter 5

THE CULTURAL REVOLUTION

During the middle and late 1960s, cracks in the Chinese Communist Party widened. Some Chinese leaders felt that Mao Tse-tung was moving too rashly, both at home and abroad. They pushed for more cautious policies.

Mao made his bid to regain control of the party with the Great Proletarian (Working People's) Cultural Revolution. It was launched in 1966 by the Red Guards, a national organization of teenagers and young adults organized by Mao. They were pledged to uphold the "purity of Mao Tse-tung revolutionary thought."

The Red Guards charged that many teachers, party officials, and others in high places were "taking the capitalist road" instead of "trusting the masses." They saw a new, educated elite of would-be mandarins forming in China. It was the job of the proletariat, or workers and farmers, to root out "old" ideas and customs. The Red Guards, with Mao's support, set out to change the beliefs of the whole of society.

Chairman Liu Shao-ch'i was one of the earliest and most powerful victims of the Cultural Revolution. By the close of 1967, he and his wife had been denounced throughout China. They were humiliated in Red Guards meetings and trials and were stripped of office. Liu vanished from the public eye in the late 1960s. He reportedly died of pneumonia while under detention.

Huge handwritten posters ("big-character posters") were the newspapers of the Cultural Revolution. Individuals and groups wrote out their charges against "those in authority taking the capitalist road" and tacked them up in public places for all to see.

Great debates were held to sort out different views among the masses, and to isolate and correct the thinking of people who still clung to old ideas and practices. Those who seemed too heavily influenced by Western culture were also attacked.

The official line was that reason, not force, should be used to resolve differences. Yet the Red Guards stormed party offices and seized universities and schools. They demonstrated and sometimes rioted in support of "Mao Tse-tung Thought." Some "capitalist roaders" received sound thrashings, or worse, at the hands of the Red Guards. Many died, and millions more suffered humiliation, torture, or the hardships of reform through labor. Bands of youths went on "Long Marches" in the countryside to spread the Cultural Revolution and to learn from the masses.

By 1969, Mao was again in complete control of the party. Chiang Ch'ing (Jiang Qing), Mao's wife, rose rapidly within party ranks. But the Red Guards grew to be a serious problem. Mao finally had to send the Red Army to rein in the movement in 1969.

The man at the head of the Red Army was Lin Piao (Lin Biao). Born in Hupeh (Hubei) Province in 1907, Lin graduated from the Whampoa Military Academy. As a teen he fought in the Northern Expedition against the warlords. Lin met Mao Tse-tung in 1928,

"Big-character posters" that looked much like this were the newspapers of the Cultural Revolution.

QUOTATIONS FROM CHAIRMAN MAO TSE-TUNG

"A revolution is not a dinner party....A revolution is an insurrection, an act of violence by which one class overthrows another." (1927)

"We have always maintained that the revolution must rely on the masses of the people, on everybody's taking a hand, and have opposed relying merely on a few persons issuing orders." (1948)

"Dust will accumulate if a room is not cleaned regularly, our faces will get dirty if they are not washed regularly. Our comrades' minds and our Party's work may also collect dust, and also need sweeping and washing." (1945)

"Not to have a correct political point of view is like having no soul." (1957)

"In any society in which classes exist, class struggle will never end. In a classless society the struggle between the new and the old and between truth and falsehood will never end." (1964)

"What we demand is the unity of politics and art, and unity of content and form, the unity of revolutionary political content and the highest possible perfection of artistic form." (1942)

when he joined the Communist forces. In 1932, Lin took command of the First Army and led it on the Long March.

Lin almost died of wounds suffered in the war against the Japanese. He spent five years recovering in the hospital. But the 1946-49 civil war saw him back in action again, as a leader of the Fourth Field Army. In 1959 he was named minister of defense.

During the next several years, Lin took to calling Mao Tse-tung a genius. The chairman's ideas, said Lin, were "lasting truth." In the late 1960s, Lin worked closely with Chiang Ch'ing, Mao's wife and cultural adviser to the army. Mao called on Lin and the army to restore order in 1969, when the Cultural Revolution exploded out of control. That same year, a new constitution named Lin Piao as the heir to Mao Tse-tung.

But the tide turned for Lin in 1970. Mao feared that the army was getting too powerful. An official report claimed that Lin participated in a plot to kill Mao in September of 1971. Lin was said to have died in a plane crash while trying to flee to the Soviet Union.

Though the fighting was over, the ideas and practices of the Cultural Revolution lingered for years. The movement disrupted industry and the transportation and communication systems. Agriculture was also affected.

Universities were closed from 1966 to 1970. When they reopened they were under the management of Revolutionary Committees consisting of workers, party members, and army members. These committees decided what was to be taught and who was to receive a university education. Courses were shortened, and education was combined with productive labor. Before being considered for advanced study, a young person had to spend two years in the countryside, working with and learning from farmers and other workers. Groups of workers decided who among them would go to college. Correct views on politics and work were as important to a candidate as good grades. The purpose of education, said Chairman Mao, was to serve the people.

The Cultural Revolution affected every aspect of Chinese existence—literature, the arts, and even family life were transformed to conform with Mao Tse-tung's ideas. Mao's leadership again was unchallenged; it remained so until 1976, the year of his death.

FOREIGN POLICY

The split with the Soviet Union widened in the late 1960s. By 1969, there were serious border clashes between Russia and China along the Ussuri River. High-level talks failed to resolve the differences. The fighting stopped, but both nations maintained huge armies along the border. They also competed for influence among the developing nations, particularly in Asia and Africa. Both sides sent aid to Communist forces fighting in Vietnam and other Southeast Asian countries.

Communist China's relations with the United States had been unfriendly from the beginning. The two countries had never exchanged ambassadors. The United States maintained that Chiang Kai-shek's Nationalist government on Taiwan was the only legitimate government of the Chinese people. America sent Chiang billions of dollars in economic and military aid. China's seat in the United Nations was held by a representative of the Taiwan-based Republic of China, not the mainland People's Republic.

The Nanking high school students shown above are playing table tennis, a favorite sport of Chinese young people. In the spring of 1971, China, in its first gesture of friendship in more than twenty years, invited a United States table-tennis team (left) to visit the People's Republic. It was the first step in China's new "Ping-Pong diplomacy."

The Communist Chinese said that until America withdrew its support from the Nationalists on Taiwan, diplomatic relations were impossible. For the most part, Chinese diplomacy in the 1950s and 1960s ignored the United States—and vice versa. Instead, the Chinese concentrated on improving relations with other nations, especially Third World countries (the developing nations of Africa, Asia, and Latin America).

The picture began to change in 1969. United States President Richard M. Nixon lifted some of the travel and trade restrictions that had been in force since 1950. Support for recognizing the People's Republic was growing in the United Nations, despite continuing United States opposition.

In April, 1971, China made a dramatic move. The government invited a United States table-tennis team that was touring Japan to visit the People's Republic. It was the first gesture of friendship in more than twenty years—and the opening move in China's new "Ping-Pong diplomacy." The team was welcomed by Premier Chou En-lai and other high party officials. Games were played in Peking, Canton, and Shanghai. The Americans were warmly received everywhere they went.

Later that summer, Henry Kissinger made a secret visit to China. Kissinger was President Nixon's adviser on foreign affairs and national security. He and Premier Chou made arrangements for Nixon to visit China early in 1972.

The announcement of President Nixon's visit to China stunned the world. After all, the United States and China had no formal diplomatic relations. America had never officially recognized the Communist government.

The announcement of Nixon's visit also affected the situation at the United Nations. In a vote at the autumn, 1971, meeting,

Mao Tse-tung greets President Richard Nixon during Nixon's 1972 trip to China.

China's seat on the Security Council was given to a delegate from the People's Republic. The United States voted against the move. Nationalist China was recorded as absent.

President Nixon's trip to China in 1972 included long talks with Premier Chou En-lai, China's top diplomat. Nixon also called on Mao Tse-tung. The results of the talks were summed up in the Shanghai Communique. The paper outlined areas of agreement and disagreement between the two powers. Perhaps most important, the United States conceded that Taiwan was an integral part of China.

Following the communique, dozens of nations formally recognized the People's Republic. But the United States did not grant full recognition until 1979.

Chou En-lai

CHOU EN-LAI

Chou En-lai (Zhou Enlai) was one of the most outstanding leaders and statesmen of the Chinese Revolution. Born to a well-to-do family in Kiangsu (Jiangsu) Province in 1898, Chou studied in Japan, Germany, and France. He joined the Communist Party in 1922.

Chou served as political director of Whampoa Military Academy and was one of the three key leaders in the 1927 Shanghai workers' and peasants' uprising. He barely escaped with his life when Chiang Kai-shek began his violent anti-Communist campaign in 1927.

In May, 1933, Chou became the Communist Red Army's political commissar. He helped to lead the Long March in 1934-35 and made many important contributions to the Chinese Communist revolution.

A gifted administrator and diplomat, Chou was named premier of the People's Republic upon its founding in 1949. He also became foreign minister, a post he held until 1958. For years afterward, Chou remained the spokesman for Communist China. He led numerous missions abroad and gained the respect and admiration of many world leaders.

The huge expanse of Peking's Tien An Men Square (above) was filled with more than a million Chinese people who mourned the death of Chou En-lai on January 8, 1976.

Chou was elected to the Central Committee in the early 1950s and remained a member until his death. Though many of his peers fell from power during the Cultural Revolution, Chou weathered the storm. He stayed in office as vice-chairman of the Central Committee and premier of the State Council. His skills as an administrator were invaluable in providing a solid, practical base for the Communist revolution. More than a million Chinese people crowded into Peking's Tien An Men Square to mourn his death on January 8, 1976.

Chapter 6

1976—A CHANGE
OF COMMAND

The death of Chou En-lai launched a year of crisis for the People's Republic. Chou was the second most powerful leader in China, a gifted policymaker and brilliant diplomat. His alliance with Mao went back fifty years.

Mao himself lay near death at the age of eighty-four. So did other leaders of his generation. The founder of the Red Army, Chu Teh, died in July, 1976, at the age of ninety.

Clearly, China stood at the brink of a crisis of leadership. Who would replace the nation's founders? As if to underscore the sense of uncertainty, a major earthquake near Peking killed an estimated 750,000 people in July of 1976. Two months later, Mao Tse-tung died, on September 6, 1976.

At his death, Mao's picture hung in hundreds of millions of Chinese homes and schools, and his ideas were promoted and discussed at all levels of society. Though today's government has discouraged this sort of hero worship and criticized Mao's policies, no one denies that he was the central figure in the first quarter century of the People's Republic.

The deaths of the old leaders made room for a new cast of players. Three chief contenders for power were Teng Hsiao-p'ing (Deng Xiaoping), Hua Kuo-feng (Hua Guofeng), and Mao's widow, Chiang Ch'ing, who headed the Gang of Four, a group that supported Mao's ideas.

Teng Hsiao-p'ing was considered Chou En-lai's most likely successor. But shortly after Chou's funeral, the Gang of Four began a bitter campaign of criticism against Teng. By April, Teng was dismissed from office. Hua, who until then had played a fairly small part in Chinese politics, became acting premier.

The struggle for power seesawed for the rest of 1976. Hua and the Gang of Four were on top for a while. But Teng did not stay down for long.

THE GANG OF FOUR

The Gang of Four led the race for power as 1976 began. The group's leader, Chiang Ch'ing, was born in 1914 in Shantung Province. She had a long, colorful, and often controversial career.

Chiang became a Shanghai film actress in the 1930s. Sometime during the 1940s, she married Mao Tse-tung. By 1948 she headed the film office of the Propaganda Department. Early in the 1960s she began a revolutionary reform movement in Peking opera and ballet.

Chiang Ch'ing's star rose quickly during the Cultural Revolution. She became identified with the radical movement in Chinese politics. In February, 1966, Chiang became the army's cultural adviser. Her job was to promote Mao Tse-tung's ideas, and she did so with what many people considered to be a vengeance.

For years after the Gang of Four were removed from office, anything that went wrong in China was blamed on them. These children are drawing anti-Gang of Four posters.

Chiang's allies in the Gang of Four included Wang Hung-wen (Wang Hongwen), Chang Ch'un-ch'iao (Zhang Chunqiao), and Yao Wen-yuan (Yao Wenyuan). They were all members of the Central Committee of the Chinese Communist Party and were widely held responsible for many of the excesses of the Cultural Revolution. It is said that Chiang was behind the attacks on Teng in the early 1970s, which threw Teng from power and labeled him a "scab and a traitor."

No one moved against the Gang of Four while Mao lived. But the picture changed after his death in September.

Premier Hua Kuo-feng replaced Mao as party chairman. Early in October, 1976, the Gang of Four were arrested. Chiang was charged with plotting to become a new empress and expelled from the party. The Gang of Four were accused of "plotting to seize power and restore capitalism in China" and removed from office. For years afterward, anything that went wrong in China—from major economic problems right down to a tractor that wouldn't start—was blamed on the Gang of Four.

HUA KUO-FENG

Hua Kuo-feng (Hua Guofeng), who replaced Chairman Mao, was born in Shansi Province in 1921, the year the Chinese Communist Party was founded. His career began in the provinces, as a guerrilla leader and local party secretary. In the late 1940s and early 1950s he specialized in agricultural work.

Hua was a leader in the movement to set up cooperative farms. By 1956 he had climbed from the county to the district party level. He also shifted from farming to head the Hunan Culture and Education Office. During the next decade, he held a variety of jobs at the provincial level.

Hua advanced his political position during the Cultural Revolution and in 1971 moved to Peking to work under Chou En-lai. He was elected to the Politburo in August, 1973. Within a year and a half, Hua had become the sixth-ranking Communist in China and minister of public security.

Hua's close relationship with Mao Tse-tung helped him get the support he needed to emerge as Mao's successor. By October of 1976, Hua had become the first person in Chinese Communist history to hold the top army, government, and party posts at the same time. He was chief of the armed forces, premier, and party chairman. Hua's rule did not last long, however. Teng Hsiao-p'ing leapfrogged back into power in 1977, and Hua's fortunes began to decline.

TENG HSIAO-P'ING

By the mid-1980s, Teng Hsiao-p'ing (Deng Xiaoping) had been in and out of power as many times as the last emperor of China was on and off the throne. Born in Szechwan Province in 1904, Teng studied in France in 1920 and joined the Chinese Communist Party in 1924. He worked with army units in the southwest during the 1930s and 1940s and transferred to Peking in 1952.

Teng rose rapidly through party ranks. He was elected to the Politburo in 1955. A year later he joined the Standing Committee and became the party's general secretary. He played an important role in China's split with the Soviet Union in the early 1960s. But early in the Cultural Revolution, Teng was arrested. He lost all his titles—everything, in fact, except his party membership.

By 1973, however, Teng was back in office. This time he headed the army, and also held government and party posts directly under Chou En-lai. Teng was secure while Chou lived. But three months after Chou's death in January, 1976, Teng's enemies in the radical wing of the Politburo threw him out of office a second time. That's when Hua Kuo-feng became acting premier. Hua and the Gang of Four seemingly enjoyed the blessing of the aging Chairman Mao. But Mao died in September, 1976, and in the next month of that fast-moving year, the Gang of Four were arrested. By July, 1977, Teng had recaptured all his former posts.

A CONTEST OF IDEAS

The battle for power in 1976 and 1977 was a contest of ideas as well as of politicians. At issue was how to balance the desire for true equality among all citizens with the goal of transforming China into a modern industrial state. The Gang of Four, Hua, and Teng all wanted the best for China. But they lined up in different places on the seesaw of ideas.

Broadly speaking, the Gang of Four stressed the importance of the Communist ideal of a classless society. They were deeply suspicious of Western ideas and what they viewed as capitalist corruption. The Chinese people, they felt, should move forward together. No one group should advance ahead of the rest. During the Cultural Revolution's great debate on whether it was better to be "Red" or "expert," the radicals definitely favored Redness.

Under the Gang of Four, millions of students left their schools during the Cultural Revolution and went to the countryside to work with and learn from the peasants. Teachers, artists, scientists, and highly skilled people were put to work feeding hogs and cleaning rest rooms. Group solutions to problems were the rule, with all voices equal. Mao Tse-tung's writings were consulted whenever a question arose.

Teng Hsiao-p'ing placed more emphasis on the need to modernize China. One can be expert and Red, too, he said. A loyal Communist, Teng nonetheless felt that China could learn from the West. To modernize close to a fourth of the world's population, China could not afford to waste native talent or refuse help from—and trade with—capitalist countries.

Hua's views fell closer to the Gang's. But in the year following Mao Tse-tung's death, Teng Hsiao-p'ing prevailed.

MODERNIZATION

In February of 1978, Teng and his followers announced a new Ten-Year Plan. It called for a program of Four Modernizations. Industry, agriculture, science, and defense were all to be improved.

Teng emerged as the top leader of post-Mao China. In January,

The White Swan Hotel in Canton is one of China's new luxury hotels built to accommodate foreign visitors.

1979, he became the first major Chinese Communist leader to visit the United States. That same month, the United States and the People's Republic recognized each other formally and opened full diplomatic relations. After that, relations between the two countries improved steadily. Restrictions in travel were lifted, and Chinese-American trade increased dramatically. Some 40,000 American tourists visited China in 1980. Four years later the number rose to 145,000.

Luxury hotels sprouted in Peking, Shanghai, and other major Chinese cities to accommodate the rising tide of visitors from the United States, European countries, and Japan. In the early 1980s, Peking's $75 million Great Wall Hotel charged $90 a day and up for rooms, with a VIP suite for $800 a day. The hotel featured nine restaurants, a swimming pool, health spa, tennis courts, and a sky lounge for dancing. Nanking's new Jinling Hotel became the tallest building in China, at thirty-seven stories. American

Teng Hsiao-p'ing

investors paid for construction of these two hotels, and foreign capital was being sought to finance dozens of other similar ventures.

Meanwhile, Teng moved to consolidate his leadership. Chiang Ch'ing was sentenced to death in January, 1981, but was given two years to reform before the sentence would be carried out. In a dramatic courtroom scene, Chiang swore she would never change her views. When the death sentence was pronounced, she shouted, "Making revolution is no crime!" She was handcuffed and dragged from the courtroom. In 1983 Chiang's sentence was changed to life in prison.

Hua Kuo-feng was eased from office in 1981, the same year that a reassessment of Mao's ideas was carried out by the party's Central Committee. The official line became: Mao was a great leader who made some bad mistakes in his last years.

Much of Teng's work in the early 1980s aimed at correcting what he viewed as Mao's errors. Under Teng's leadership, peasants were allowed to engage in limited private enterprise. Teng changed the rules for admitting students to college to place more stress on aptitude for advanced study. He shifted China's economic emphasis to producing consumer goods, and he made state-run industry more accountable for profit and loss. Teng also launched a massive program to limit Chinese families to one child each.

These moves angered many party members who believed in Mao's ideas. To them, private enterprise meant competition, while communism meant cooperation and sharing. Mao had scoffed at warnings of a population explosion, saying that more people in the labor force would strengthen China's self-reliance. Yet Teng was telling families not to have more than one child. In cities where Chinese workers were lucky to have 40 square feet (3.71 square meters) of living space with no hot water or private toilet, Teng was building fancy hotels where foreigners were served by waiters in tuxedos.

Teng spent much effort to quiet the grumbling and to convince people to accept his views. First, he put friends in high places to carry out his policies. Hu Yao-pang (Hu Yaobang), Teng's top lieutenant, became the party's general secretary. Chao Chi-yang (Zhao Ziyang) was named premier. Teng was the most powerful political figure in the country. He became head of the Central Advisory Commission as well as the government and party military commissions.

By 1982 Teng was strong enough to launch a massive government reshuffling. Top ministers were replaced, and China adopted a new constitution. Teng continued his policy of expanding China's free-market economy. He began to dismantle the system of rural communes that Mao had founded twenty-five years before. Under Teng's policy of "individual responsibility," workers and farmers were allowed to keep some of the profits of increased production.

Though Teng's reforms had top-level support, there was a good deal of resistance to his policies at local party and government levels. Much of it centered in the 10 million people who joined the Communist Party during the Cultural Revolution, when Mao's ideas reigned supreme. In 1983, Teng launched a three-year campaign to rid the party of some 3 to 5 million Maoists. These people had held on to their posts largely on the basis of favors exchanged with friends in other government and party jobs. Teng felt they were undermining his reforms, and he accused them of responsibility for government waste and corruption. The campaign's goal was reeducation: "curing the illness to save the patient," as Hu Yao-pang put it. Maoists who failed to reform their ideas were to be ousted from the party.

In another campaign launched in 1983, Teng declared war on Western culture. While it was important to move ahead on modernizing China's economy, Teng said, "On no account should we learn and import the capitalist system and its hideous and decadent ideology and culture."

By the mid-1980s, Teng's policies seemed responsible for increased production and improved living standards, especially in certain parts of the countryside. Whether Teng would succeed in quieting or winning over his critics remained to be seen. Teng, in his eighties, seemed bent on assuring that his reforms would outlive him.

While China and the United States drew closer together,

Chinese relations with the Soviet Union showed little improvement. The two major Communist powers, along with the United States, continued to compete for influence among the underdeveloped nations of the Third World. Chinese troops clashed with Russian-supplied Vietnamese forces along the China-Vietnam border. The Chinese supported Cambodian forces in an armed struggle against the Vietnamese. The Chinese and Russians held a round of talks in Moscow in March, 1984, to seek an improved relationship. But China said that until the Soviet Union pulled out of Afghanistan, stopped supporting Vietnam, and withdrew Russian troops from the Chinese border, progress would be impossible.

By 1980 China had become a major world power. No one could predict the outcome of its foreign policy or tell when new leaders might turn China in a different direction. One thing was certain: The actions of the People's Republic, both within its borders and outside them, would have a major impact on the rest of the world for years to come.

THE POLITICAL SYSTEM TODAY

There are three major political organizations in Communist China—the party, the army, and the government. In fact, the real power rests with the Chinese Communist Party. The party decides policy. The army and government carry out the party's decisions.

With about 40 million members, the Chinese Communist Party is the largest in the world. Still, only about one of every twenty-five Chinese is a party member—the smallest percentage of any Communist country. To join the party, a citizen must apply in writing, pass an exam, and be sponsored by two party members.

Communists hold all the key positions in the government and the army. They also play leading roles in schools, farms, and factories.

Local Communists elect representatives to one of twenty-nine Provincial Party Committees. These committees, in turn, send representatives to the National Party Congress, held about every five years. The congress elects a Central Committee of about two hundred members. These people do the routine work of the party. The twenty-seven members of the Central Committee's Politburo (Political Bureau) are the most powerful group in China. The Politburo elects a Standing Committee and a Secretariat, which actually decide policy for the entire country. The chairman of the Standing Committee is the real head of the Chinese government.

According to the 1979 constitution, the National People's Congress (not the same as the National Party Congress) is the only legislative authority in the country. In practice, the National People's Congress has very few powers. Its main job is to rubber-stamp decisions made by the Chinese Communist Party. Delegates to the National People's Congress are elected at the provincial level from a list drawn up by the party. On the advice of the party, the delegates appoint the members of the State Council, which oversees the government ministries and bureaus.

The Communist Party, through the Central Military Council, also oversees the army. Whoever heads the council is the chief of the armed forces. The People's Liberation Army (PLA) is probably the second most important organization in China. Every year about 750,000 young men and women are called up for service of from three to six years. There are 3 to 4 million soldiers in the PLA. They undergo political, as well as military, training.

Members of the People's Liberation Army play an active role in

People's Liberation Army soldiers play an active role in the working life of China.

the working life of the country. They regularly are sent to farms and factories to help with flood control, harvesting, and other projects. Army units dig ditches and canals for the people and try to work their own farms, so as not to burden their neighbors.

Women soldiers have the same responsibilities as men. Opportunities for women are increasing in the PLA, as elsewhere in China. Recently a class of women pilots graduated from flying school.

Most Chinese workers and farmers receive military training from the PLA. The idea behind the People's Militia (citizens' army) is to make every worker a soldier, ready to fight alongside the PLA, if necessary. Likewise, every PLA soldier is supposed to be a worker.

It's a great honor to be a PLA member. A soldier's family receives a red and yellow plaque proclaiming it to be a "Glorious Army Family." At mass meetings each Army Day (August 1), PLA families are singled out for praise.

Most urban workers in China live in traditional two- or three-room houses (above) or crowded apartment buildings (left).

Chapter 7

CITY LIFE

The People's Republic has thirty-one cities with estimated populations of over 1 million—more than any other country in the world. About 100 million of the total Chinese work force of 406 million earn their living in cities or suburbs.

Until very recently, city workers were generally better off than rural workers. City workers had better housing, as a rule. They enjoyed a wider choice of food, consumer goods, and entertainment. Early in the 1980s, rural workers began to catch up economically, and the gap between city and country was closing fast. Moreover, city workers faced certain problems that didn't apply to rural workers. Many factories were noisy and dusty, with out-of-date equipment. Work places were not heated in winter or cooled in summer. Air pollution levels were high in many Chinese cities.

As the 1980s began, most urban workers lived in two- or three-room houses and apartments. Some shared a kitchen and bath with one or more families. Water often came from a communal tap. Furnishings were simple—a bed for each family member, a table, a few chairs, and perhaps a wardrobe or a few trunks. Under the so-called individual responsibility system, radios,

Many people in China's cities gather in parks and squares in the early morning to perform tai chi chuan, *an ancient series of exercise movements.*

television sets, sewing machines, and other consumer goods were starting to appear.

Where jobs were available, everyone in the family worked except students, old people, and anyone who was sick. After a predawn breakfast of cereal and vegetables, the workers might exercise at a city park. Most people worked eight hours a day, six days a week.

Production targets set for each worker were usually fairly low. In general, factory work was not as hard as farm work. City workers who produced more than their quotas earned a bonus.

For years, the average salary in a state-run factory was between thirty and forty-five *yuan* a month. (In 1984 there were roughly two *yuan* to the United States dollar.) Rent for a family apartment came to about five *yuan* a month. Two meals a day at a factory ran about fifteen *yuan* a month. After the late 1970s, when Teng

Among the millions of people who are part of China's private business sector are this outdoor dentist in Chungking (left) and the owner of this street cafe in Wuhan (right).

Hsiao-p'ing came to power, the individual responsibility system produced dramatic changes in Chinese life. Workers were urged to produce more and thereby earn and keep more money for themselves. As a result, in less than a decade, the average monthly wage in state-run factories rose to about seventy-five *yuan*.

Even more important was the rapid development of a private business sector to supplement China's planned economy. Between 1978 and 1982, the number of licensed private businesses in China multiplied by thirty. By 1984, nearly 3.25 million people were engaged in licensed private industrial and commercial enterprises. Hundreds of restaurants in the major cities provided welcome relief from the drab food served in state-run canteens. Private shops repaired everything from bicycles to television sets. People began to work privately as tailors, cooks, maids, and nannies— occupations unheard of in the days of Mao Tse-tung.

The *getihu*, China's new entrepreneurs, had to give up welfare, housing assignments, and pension benefits to work for profit. Some were beaten and harassed by jealous state workers and die-hard Maoists. Nonetheless, the rewards could be great. At the age of only twenty-one, Fu Ji, manager of a five-table restaurant in Peking, was netting between one hundred and two hundred *yuan* a month after taxes.

In Teng's China, it became politically correct "to make some people rich first, so as to lead all the people to wealth." Private enterprise, it was argued, would increase production, and more production was what China needed to modernize. The new policies also were designed to deal with growing unemployment.

Teng's policies increased earnings for the average city worker and created new jobs. They also produced some undesirable results. Taxes on private businesses, intended to finance the overall economy, proved hard to collect. Tax fraud and evasion became widespread. The Chinese had no system to regulate private enterprise. In the Peking city government, fewer than sixty people administered and regulated all the city's private retailers in 1983. Yet more than seven thousand licenses for private businesses were issued in Peking in the first four months of that year alone.

Growing numbers of state employees began to play hooky from their factory jobs to run their own businesses—many of them unlicensed. As incomes rise, so does the demand for consumer goods, from better food and clothes to bicycles and television sets. In China in the mid-1980s, those goods were hard to come by legally. There were long waiting lists for bicycles, and cotton was rationed. A worker could buy only about six yards of material for a year's clothing, including sheets and bedding.

To meet the demand for consumer goods, illegal trade began to mushroom. Profiteers charged high prices for goods stolen from state factories or smuggled in from outside China. Ironically, the policy of encouraging people to acquire wealth helped to create an environment in which criminals could flourish. While the average urban family was probably better off than ever before by 1984, it remained to be seen whether those who got rich would be willing to lead the rest of the people to wealth.

PEKING

No other city in the People's Republic shows the contrast between ancient and modern China as well as does Peking (Beijing), the capital. Known as the Garden City of the World because of its many parks, Peking is really several cities in one.

Peking was founded by Mongol emperor Kublai Khan in the late 1200s. The fabulous palaces of the Forbidden City were begun by the Ming in the 1400s, though most of the buildings standing today date from the seventeenth and eighteenth centuries. These former imperial dwellings cover 250 acres (101 hectares) in the heart of Peking. Once, no one was allowed to enter the grounds without permission. Today the Forbidden City is open to all.

Five marble bridges cross the Golden Water Stream and lead to the heart of the Forbidden City. The Hall of Supreme Harmony, where little P'u Yi became China's last emperor, stands on a three-tiered terrace edged by three carved marble railings. Pairs of bronze storks and tortoises guard the entrance. The walls are deep red, and the hall is topped by a gold-tiled roof. Inside the hall, the central columns are carved with dragons and covered with gold.

Many other magnificent buildings lie within the Forbidden City, which is surrounded by a moat and high walls. The ancient city of Peking once sprawled around this imperial hub and was in turn protected by steep walls. But most of them have been torn down to make way for the new Peking.

Directly south of the Forbidden City, through the Gate of Heavenly Peace, lies Tien An Men Square. Covering almost 100 acres (40 hectares), the square is the heart of modern Peking.

On the square's west side stands the Great Hall of the People, where the National People's Congress meets. The Chinese built it in ten months—561,800 square feet (52,193 square meters) of conference rooms, banquet halls, and reception areas. South of the Gate of Heavenly Peace stands the granite and marble Monument to the People's Heroes. Behind the monument stands Chairman Mao Tse-tung Memorial Hall, where Mao's preserved body lies in state and a large marble statue of him dominates the building. In 1983 the government announced that Mao's remains and statue would be joined by statues of other heroes, including Premier Chou En-lai.

People get around in Peking by bicycle, electric trolley bus, subway, and of course, on foot. State taxis and minibuses carry foreign guests. A few private cars were starting to appear in the 1980s.

Chang An Boulevard, one of the widest streets in the world, runs east and west at the south end of Tien An Men Square. Other main streets divide Peking into residential and business sections.

Narrow lanes crisscross older parts of the city, where people live in adobe-style houses behind gray stone walls. In newer, rebuilt sections, the streets are wider and are lined with trees and apartment buildings.

Peking's Chang An Boulevard (above) is one of the widest streets in the world. Most of the city's residents use bicycles for transportation (below). The granite and marble Monument to the People's Heroes (left) stands in front of Chairman Mao Tse-tung Memorial Hall in Tien An Men Square.

A busy Peking street corner

Life is fairly quiet in the residential areas—quiet, that is, for a city of nine million people. But Peking's business sections bustle. Food stalls sell tea and snacks of bean cake or noodles. In the marketplaces, people shop for fresh fruits and vegetables. Small, crowded shops sell everything from pottery to books, as do large department stores. Outer parts of the city hold tall government buildings, factories, and modern housing.

Neighborhood groups, mostly elderly people, visit the sick, run clinics, and conduct health classes in all parts of the city. They provide family planning information and have been largely responsible for the success of the government's "one child per family" policy, at least in urban areas.

Peking is an athletic city. The February Spring Festival is an annual event. Three thousand runners gather in Tien An Men Square for a footrace around the city. No prizes are given, but it's

Peking soup stands such as this one (left) usually do a brisk business.
Even the narrow back streets of this capital city are crowded (right).

a great honor for men, women, and teenagers simply to take part.
In June, the Workers' Stadium hosts a track and field meet.
Athletes from all over the country are there to share their skills
with others. Exercise and sports are an important part of Chinese
life.

Throughout Peking, people gather in the early morning before
work to perform *tai chi chuan*. This ancient series of movements
exercises every part of the body. It is designed to bring each
individual into harmony with nature. *Tai chi chuan* is especially
popular with older Chinese men and women.

Ping-Pong, soccer, and basketball are favorite sports of Chinese
children. In Peking's schools, exercise periods are a regular part of
every school day. The Physical Training Institute offers special
coaching to children from all over China who excel at sports.

Peking is also a center for higher learning. Peking University,

95

Qin Hua University, and the Peking Languages Institute are three of the more than thirty colleges, universities, and technical schools in the city. In the early 1980s a few private colleges opened their doors.

Visitors flock to Peking's Museum of Chinese History to see the life-size terra-cotta soldiers and horses that were excavated from an ancient tomb. Peking houses a number of other fine museums, including the Palace Garden Museum, which contains many treasures from the past; the Museum of the Revolution; the National Art Gallery; and the Lu Hsün (Lu Xun) Museum, named after the great revolutionary writer. The pandas at the Peking Zoo are a favorite attraction for natives and foreigners alike.

Until modern times, crime was not a major problem in Peking and other major Chinese cities. But theft, assault, and other crimes increased after the Cultural Revolution disrupted millions of lives between 1966 and 1976. Many schools shut down during the late sixties. When they reopened, standards were generally lower. Millions of young people had gone to the countryside to spread the Cultural Revolution. When they returned to seek work in the cities, many lacked the skills required for good jobs. Nearly twenty million people were out of work in the mid-1980s. Finding jobs for them was a major challenge facing the government.

SHANGHAI

With a population of nearly twelve million, Shanghai is the largest and most densely populated city in the world. Overlooking a bend in the Huang Po, or Yellow River (not the same as the great Yellow River to the north), it is China's most important seaport.

Shanghai is China's most important seaport.

European-style buildings along the shoreline once housed Western banks and trading companies. Zhongshan Road, a boulevard with narrow gardens, lines the riverbank. From it, Nanjing Road runs past the Peace Hotel and into the most Westernized shopping area in China. Nowhere is the Chinese appetite for consumer goods more apparent than in Shanghai. Displays of fancy portable radios, colorful blouses, and late-model television sets attract hordes of window shoppers.

Shanghai is a major center of trade and industry. Its people are better off than most other Chinese. In Shanghai one is likely to see ribbons in a girl's hair, or a young couple holding hands. These sights would be shocking in many other parts of China.

Shanghai's Suzhou (Wusong) River (above) runs through the city and empties into the larger Huang Po (Yellow River).

In older sections of the city, people still live along narrow lanes in run-down housing—some without running water. Every house has electricity, though often only enough to power a light bulb.

Farther from the city center, modern industry employs an army of skilled workers. The factories around Shanghai produce everything from electronics to textiles, iron and steel, cars, machinery, tires, paper, and glassware. Shipbuilding and oil refining are other important industries. But there are few natural resources in the immediate area. Shanghai receives its raw materials by train or boat from elsewhere in China.

In the newer industrial sections, modern, three-story apartment houses surround each factory. Every district has its own schools, hospitals, shopping center, and parks.

Beyond the suburbs, farms supply the city with fresh vegetables, grain, and other food. But the sight of the low hills to the west is often clouded by air pollution.

Shanghai scenes

These views of Canton include
a house and private garden (above),
newspaper sellers (left), and
a busy intersection (below).

CANTON

Canton

About a quarter of China's foreign trade is carried on at two giant fairs held in Canton (Guangzhou) each spring and fall. The Chinese Export Commodities Fairs attract tens of thousands of foreign business people. In fact, Canton has been an important trade center for two thousand years. Records show that Roman traders visited the city during the Han dynasty (202 B.C.-A.D. 221).

Canton lies on a bend of the Pearl River. Its port, Whampoa, is the major foreign trade port for southern China. Local industry includes sugar refineries, paper mills, and cement, fertilizer, and chemical plants.

In the early 1900s, Canton was a miserable place. Filth and disease were widespread among miles and miles of makeshift houses. Much of the city was pulled down in the 1920s, and later the Communists continued to modernize Canton. Today it is a lovely tropical city with many parks and long, treelined streets. The population exceeds two million.

One of the oldest buildings in China sits on a hilltop in Yue Xiu Park. A five-story tower that dates from the fourteenth century, it once served as a watchtower. Today it is a museum of treasures from the Han period through the revolution.

In the 1800s, Sha Mian Island held tennis courts, a sailing club, and a soccer field for the British and French consulates. By the early 1900s, hundreds of foreigners lived on the island. Today the fine old buildings have fallen on hard times. Two former churches have been converted into a printing plant and an office building.

The Peasant Movement Institute occupies a former temple of Confucius. Built in the sixteenth century, the temple became a training center for Communists in the 1920s. Mao Tse-tung, Chou

Many Wuhan residents live in crowded two-story housing and shop for food at outdoor markets.

En-lai, and other leaders worked there until 1927, when the Nationalists drove them out. Today Mao's office and bedroom have been restored, along with lecture rooms, the dining hall, and former student dormitories.

The Canton Zoo is one of the largest in China. The city also has a fine observatory. Zhong Shan University offers liberal arts and natural science training, plus a first-rate medical school. On Sundays, soccer matches draw crowds to the university's outdoor stadium.

WUHAN AND OTHER INDUSTRIAL CITIES

Wuhan, an industrial center on the Yangtze River southwest of Shanghai, is really three cities: Wuchang, Hankou, and Hanyang. In ancient times, Wuchang was a thriving cultural center. Today it contains an important medical and agricultural college. Hankou was built by the British in the 1800s. Many of its people live in crowded, two-story wooden shacks. In the summer they cook, eat,

Wuhan's steel plant is the second largest in the People's Republic.

and wash their clothes outdoors. The steel plant in Hanyang employs about 65,000 workers. Built by the Russians, who abandoned it in 1960, the plant is the second largest in the People's Republic.

Haerh-pin and Shenyang (Mukden) are two important industrial centers in the northeast. Coal from Fushun fuels the textile mills, factories, and machine-tool shops in Shenyang. Fushun's open-pit mine is the largest in the world. The town's houses are built around the edge of the pit. Nearby Anshan contains China's largest iron-smelting plant.

Tientsin (Tianjin), Peking's seaport, also turns out bicycles, tractors, and diesel engines. Chungking (Chongqing), on the Yangtze River, manufactures electrical equipment and machine tools.

SHOWCASE CITIES—NANKING, SUCHOU, HANGCHOU

To the west of Nanking (Nanjing) lies the Yangtze River; to the east, the Purple Mountains (Ze Jin). This lovely site has been inhabited since 4000 B.C. At several times in Chinese history, Nanking was the nation's capital. Parts of the old town walls still stand, built by the Ming in the fourteenth century.

103

The Yangtze River bridge at Nanking

The bridge over the Yangtze at Nanking is spectacular. Experts said it couldn't be built. More than 4 miles (6.4 kilometers) long, it is a double-decker bridge with four traffic lanes on the upper deck and two railway lines on the lower.

According to an old Chinese proverb, "In heaven there is paradise; on earth, Suchou and Hangchou." Favorites of the emperors, these two cities have long been considered the loveliest in China.

Suchou (Suzhou), the "Venice of the People's Republic," lies about 50 miles (80 kilometers) west of Shanghai. The area's many lakes and ponds are connected by a network of canals. The many lesser canals of the town itself eventually join the Grand Canal, which was built by Kublai Khan to carry grain from the Yangtze plain to the capital at Peking.

Suchou is not heavily industrialized. Silk spinning, weaving,

104

Suchou's many lakes and ponds are connected by a network of canals (left). For years Hangchou was famous for its silk brocades (right).

and handicrafts are the main industries. Small factories making chemicals, ceramics, and metal products have been established. Outlying regions grow rice, wheat, and tea.

The famous classic gardens of Suchou date back to the tenth century. Many of these charming and serene gardens have been carefully restored and give Suchou a beauty that is lacking in many of modern China's cities.

Hangchou (Hangzhou), southwest of Shanghai, lies on West Lake, one of the most beautiful spots in China. Three islands on the lake house pavilions, gardens, a museum, and a library.

For years the city was famous for its silk brocades. Silk is still an important industry. Tea is grown in the surrounding country, as are rice, cotton, and flax. The chemical plants, machine-tool factories, and other industries that have developed have not spoiled Hangchou's charm.

The lush countryside at Kueilin (Guilin) is a center for agriculture.

Chapter 8

RURAL LIFE

The individual responsibility system of the 1980s had as great an impact on the countryside as it had on urban life. When China began to abolish the system of rural People's Communes, some 800 million Chinese living outside the cities began trying to "get rich by working."

The new system was similar to the way the countryside was governed before the Great Leap Forward of the late 1950s. Half a dozen villages, with combined populations of around thirty-five to forty thousand, were to be administered by elected township governments. Farmers' cooperatives took over most of the economic responsibilities that had belonged to the communes.

The land is still collectively owned—that is, it belongs to the state. But under the new system it was divided into small plots privately farmed by individual households. A farm family must sell a fixed amount of grain to the state each year at a controlled price. But the family may keep the profits from anything it grows or produces in excess of its quota.

The new system produced dramatic results in a short period of time. Between 1979 and 1982, according to China's leaders, farm output grew by 7.5 percent a year—a rate twice as high as under

Farms near Canton

the commune system. The average farmer's income doubled. Since farmers could own their own homes, if not their land, many put their newfound wealth into brand-new houses. Construction in the countryside surrounding Peking rose by 25 percent between 1978 and 1982.

As was true in the cities, the government's new policy also produced some undesirable results in the countryside.

The government controlled the price of grain so that city workers could afford to buy it. But farmers could sell other crops, such as vegetables or cotton, on the free market at much higher prices. So farmers began to grow only enough grain to meet their quotas, while using the rest of their land for crops that make more money. Some planners feared that grain production, which is vital to the Chinese economy, would soon be seriously threatened.

Like city workers who were playing hooky from state jobs to

A rural worker carries a load from the fields near Kueilin.

run their own businesses, growing numbers of farmers began to leave the land to pursue greater profits elsewhere. Some bought small trucks and tractors and went into the transportation business. The millions of new small farms created a huge demand for any means of hauling crops, either to state-run markets or markets run by farmers. The Chinese soon discovered that private transportation companies often are more flexible and less expensive than state-run companies.

Chinese newspapers of the early 1980s were filled with stories of rural workers who developed unusual ways of "getting rich by working." One article told of two brothers who earned an extra five thousand *yuan* one year by trapping rats in their village and feeding the rats to ermines being raised for fur. When United States President Ronald Reagan visited China in April, 1984, the state television proudly displayed a tape of the first rural worker

A farmer moves his herd of sheep along a road near Peking.

to buy a car. A woman who got rich as a chicken farmer smiled happily and waved as she drove off in a brand new Toyota. Not all rural workers were so successful, however, and many ended up unemployed.

Crime became a growing problem in the countryside, as it had in the cities. When land was farmed collectively and everyone shared the profits, crop theft was not a problem. But when individual families began to farm their own small plots, each household had to guard its own crops. Farmers worked all day in the fields, then had to stay up all night in little guard shacks. In some places, organized gangs roamed the countryside, attacking guards and taking what they wanted.

The countryside also soon had its share of "economic criminals." In the old commune system, buying and selling were regulated through official government purchasing agents. Under the individual responsibility system, a new class of middlemen appeared. They helped rural workers and businesses make deals, charging a percentage for each purchase or sale. In parts of the country, these middlemen soon grew so powerful they could charge protection money for allowing a person to transport goods over a certain route or get into a certain business.

Private enterprise in the countryside began to undermine certain projects that once had been planned and executed by communes. Individual households, for example, simply have no resources to build a dam or flood-control project. In some parts of the country, rural workers began taking dams apart and using the bricks to build houses.

Overgrazing soon became a serious problem in sheep and cattle farming areas, such as Mongolia. When peasants owned the herds in common, the grass was plentiful. But with each family trying to

THE KANG

Housing in China ranges from mud-brick walls and packed-dirt floors to modern, two-story houses. The kang is a feature of many Chinese homes. It is a long brick platform with a hollow space beneath, connected by vent to the kitchen oven. Hot air flows through the hollow space beneath the kang and warms it before passing out through the chimney. During the cold months, all the members of a family sleep on the platform, wrapped in comforters.

breed as many animals as possible to increase herd size, much of the area began to turn to desert. In the spring, strong winds carry so much dust that people cannot see or breathe when they go outside.

In the commune system, retired people who had no families could live in "homes of respect" run by the brigade. Young people cooked for them, fetched water, and looked after their needs. The Teng government seemed to lack a comprehensive welfare policy. Official newspapers ran stories about "help the poor" groups organized by township governments, or wealthy people helping out unfortunate neighbors. But no one could predict what would happen to the increasing numbers of entrepreneurs giving up pension benefits on leaving state jobs or collective farming to start their own businesses.

China's peasants were communized, then decollectivized, in the twenty-five years between 1959 and 1984. No matter what system eventually prevails, they have a massive job to do. A population four times the size of the United States' must be fed on about two thirds as much farmland. Improved output was largely due to increased use of fertilizers and better irrigation, combined with new incentives to "get rich by working." But some scientists worry about burning out the soil through overfarming. The long-

Much of China's land is still farmed by primitive methods. Hand tools are used for cultivation and plows are pulled by men and women or by water buffalo.

range planning needed to head off such problems used to be done by the communes. Whether the new farmers' collectives would pay attention to larger land-use issues remained to be seen.

Rural life is not easy. Though China is modernizing, much of the land is still farmed by methods that have been used for centuries. Such hard labor takes its toll. Men retire at sixty; women at fifty-five, sometimes earlier. Still, no one would argue that the common people are better off than at any other time in Chinese history.

Faces of China

Chapter 9
THE CHINESE PEOPLE

There is as much variety among the people who live in China as there is in the landscape. The majority belong to a group who call themselves the Han people, after the famous dynasty founded in 202 B.C. But 6 percent of the population are minority tribes whose languages, customs, and ways of life are different from the Han majority. Though their numbers are relatively small, the national minorities are in fact the majority in China's vast frontier — that is, in more than half the country.

Most of China's national minorities live in five autonomous, or self-governing, regions along the northern, western, and southern borders. In Yunnan Province there are some twenty-five different groups. In all, fifty-four national minority groups have been identified. About ten of these have populations of more than a million each.

The Mongols comprise one of the largest national minorities. In the thirteenth century, their ancestors swept down from the north and eventually occupied all of China. Their great leader, Kublai Khan, set up his capital at Peking. After his death, Mongol power declined.

Today a few million Mongols live along China's northern borders — in Inner Mongolia (Nei Monggol) Autonomous Region and neighboring Kansu (Gansu) and Heilungkiang (Heilongjiang) provinces. Their culture and language are quite different from that of the Han Chinese. For centuries Mongols have lived as nomadic herders of sheep, cattle, and horses. They are a proud, tough, and independent people who tend to scorn the more settled way of life in China proper. They still cling to their belief in Lama Buddhism—a religion shared by the Tibetans, another large national minority group.

Some three million Tibetans live in Szechwan (Sichuan) and Tsinghai (Qinghai) provinces and in Tibet (Xizang) Autonomous Region. About 80 percent are farmers. The rest are nomads who wander the northern plateaus herding sheep and yaks.

Before the Communists occupied Tibet in 1950, all its land, at least in theory, belonged to the Dalai Lama. He is the spiritual leader of Lama Buddhism, an ancient religion that combines Buddhist beliefs with native beliefs in evil spirits, magic, and spirits of nature. The Tibetans revolted against Communist rule in 1959, and the Dalai Lama fled to India along with about 100,000 refugees. In the 1960s and 1970s, the Communists mounted a huge campaign to persuade Tibetans to give up Lama Buddhism. They systematically destroyed Tibetan monasteries and shipped some 100,000 political prisoners to labor camps. Teng reversed this policy in the 1980s and tried, unsuccessfully, to persuade the Dalai Lama to return. But it is unlikely that the Chinese Communists will loosen control over an area that is the size of western Europe and contains some 40 percent of China's mineral wealth.

Estimates of the number of Muslims in the People's Republic range from seven million to more than ten million. Among them are the Uighurs, Kazakhs, and Kirghiz of the Sinkiang (Xinjiang) Autonomous Region.

The Uighurs, though not strict in the practice of their religion, maintain contact with the rest of the Muslim world. They consider getting married and raising a family to be a religious duty. The Uighurs live by intensive farming.

The Kazakhs and Kirghiz, on the other hand, are herders of sheep, cattle, goats, and sometimes horses and camels. Some seven or eight million Kazakhs live in the Soviet Union in the Kazakh Soviet Socialist Republic. There are probably about half a million Kazakhs in China and 75,000 Kirghiz.

The Uighurs, Kazakhs, and Kirghiz write and speak Turkic languages. But the four or five million members of the Hui national minority all write and speak Chinese. Except for the fact that they are Muslims, there is little to distinguish the Hui from the Han. Though most Hui live in the Ningsia (Ningxia) Autonomous Region, some live in Yunnan, Sinkiang, and the area between Peking and Wuhan.

The Zhuang are another important ethnic group. About eight or nine million Zhuang live in the Kwangsi (Guangxi) Autonomous Region. They speak a form of Thai and live by farming rice. Westerners know very little about their religious beliefs. But it is known that the Zhuang have been absorbed to a certain extent by the Han mainstream.

More than three million Miao and about a million Yao have also adopted many features of the Han culture. These farming people live in remote mountain settlements and along streams and rivers in the southwest.

The Yi, or Lolo, still cling to many of their old customs and beliefs. Their religion is full of magic and witchcraft. The three or four million Yi are divided into clans and organized according to caste. The top castes own all the property, while those at the bottom are landless farm laborers. Yi settlements dot Yunnan, Szechwan, and Kweichow (Guizhou) provinces.

The Chinese constitution requires respect for the languages, customs, habits, and religious beliefs of the national minorities. But many of these are at odds with the principles of Chinese communism. There is another problem. Most of the national minorities live in the frontier regions. China has always felt vulnerable to attack along its long borders. The central government cannot afford to have too many doubts about the loyalty of its border people. Especially since the split with the Soviets in the early 1960s, China's policy on national minorities has been linked to its defense needs.

The government has used three main methods of influencing its border people. One is force. Another has been a mass migration of Han Chinese to the frontier. In 1969 and 1970, for example, more than a million Han settlers moved to Inner Mongolia.

A third method is education. The government publishes books, newspapers, and magazines in Mongolian, Tibetan, Uighur, Kazakh, and other minority languages. At the Institute of Nationalities in Peking, and in local schools and colleges, minority students receive Communist training. They study *putonghua*, the official language of the People's Republic, as well as works on politics and government. They practice native songs and dances. After their training they return to their communities.

As one government pamphlet put it: "It is for the different nationalities to reform of their own accord as their people raise their level of political consciousness and scientific and cultural knowledge."

Here is the official word on freedom of religion: "People of all nationalities enjoy freedom to believe in any religion, but also the freedom not to believe, and freedom to carry on propaganda for atheism. This is a fundamental right of the Chinese people of all nationalities."

Some minorities have adapted fairly readily to Chinese Communist rule. Others have resisted government efforts to "raise their level of political consciousness." In 1962, for example, nearly fifty thousand Kazakhs migrated across the border to settle with Kazakhs in the Soviet Union.

WOMEN AND THE FAMILY

Communist rule has had a profound effect on the family, as on every other aspect of Chinese life. To a certain extent, the nuclear family of parents and children has replaced the three-generation household of former times. Young people are encouraged to postpone marriage until their late twenties and to limit the size of their families.

Old attitudes die hard, however. Respect for the elderly and strong family ties are ingrained in the fabric of Chinese culture. This fact, plus a shortage of housing, tends to keep larger families together.

The marriage law of 1950 forbade arranged marriages, child brides, and bigamy. The village matchmaker and the dowry system soon vanished. To marry, a couple fills out a license and has a witness sign it. Women may keep their own names when they marry. Children take the family name of either parent.

Divorce is granted if both partners request it, and if questions of children and property are agreed on. If only one party wants a divorce, a People's Court tries to reconcile the couple's differences. If that fails, the divorce becomes final.

Communist theory calls for complete equality between the sexes. That, of course, depends on economic equality. The commune system encourages women to undertake the same share of work as men. Women are paid independently, as they are in industry. Child-care facilities make it possible for most women to work.

Chinese women are still far from the goal of complete equality. In China, as in the West, there is a strong tendency to regard domestic affairs as women's sphere and public life as men's. Only 11 percent of the two-hundred-member Central Committee of the Chinese Communist Party are women. Women generally have access to education. But it's harder for qualified women to find good jobs than it is for men. Few women, for example, become factory managers. Those who do, however, are paid the same as men.

The Federation of Women, a government organization, helps women assert their rights in the People's Republic. Other women's associations, street committees, and cultural activities help women take a full share in public life.

Population control is one of the most serious issues facing China. The country doubled in population in the thirty years after Mao's revolution. The official results of the 1982 census placed the number of Chinese at 1,031,882,511, including those in Taiwan, Hong Kong, and Macao. Half of them were under twenty-one. Even with the emphasis on limiting children, China in the 1980s had some 33,000 extra mouths to feed each day. Of the 17 million new babies each year, close to 30 percent were third or fourth children.

The government started a massive campaign to limit China's population to 1.2 billion by the year 2000. This objective will be

As part of the government's campaign to limit China's population, posters throughout the country encourage families to have only one child.

reached only if 65 percent of those under thirty limit their families to one child.

Single-child families are rewarded with income bonuses, greater health-care benefits, and better retirement pensions. Single children also get preference for day care and better jobs. Families with more than two children have to pay 10 percent of their earnings in a special tax, and they are penalized in other ways as well.

By 1984, the government's program seemed to be working better in the cities than in the countryside. Under the individual responsibility system, some peasants could earn enough to pay the penalties for extra children. And the tradition of large families remained very strong. Many parents were reluctant to limit the size of their families, especially since for centuries elderly Chinese have depended on their children's support. In any event, the success or failure of the population control campaign would have a lot to do with how well the Chinese eat in the not-too-distant future.

This painting by Yang Chih-hsien is called Exhibition Repudiating Lin Piao and Confucius.

Chapter 10

ART AND CULTURE

Mao Tse-tung's ideas on art and literature dominated the Chinese scene from the revolution until his death in 1976. Mao recognized the value of China's artistic heritage. But he also stressed the overriding importance of politics in art. The fabulous Shang bronzes, Buddhist sculptures, and other treasures of China's past were testimony, said Mao, to the skill of the working masses, even though the art was produced for the "slave-owning and feudal" ruling class.

In the years after the revolution, painters were encouraged to develop native styles and techniques. Art produced by workers, farmers, and soldiers was highly praised. Paintings idealized life in the People's Republic. Tractor drivers and oil refineries replaced such traditional subjects as long-robed scholars and waterfalls. New, revolutionary symbols replaced ancient ones. The red sun came to stand for Mao Tse-tung. A plum blossom in the snow represented early Communist martyrs.

For the first seven years of the People's Republic, artists generally supported the regime. Their morale was high. But the Hundred Flowers movement in 1957 labeled many artists "poisonous weeds" and bred a sense of insecurity that persisted into the 1980s.

Many artists had an especially hard time during the Cultural Revolution. Chiang Ch'ing and the other members of the Gang of Four conducted bitter campaigns against any form of art of which they disapproved. Art schools closed during the years from 1966 to 1976, and artists' associations were disbanded.

After the fall of the Gang of Four in October, 1976, art journals reappeared. Schools reopened, and in 1978 the National Federation of Artists and Writers was reestablished. It became acceptable to study traditional Western art. A great variety of styles appeared that would have been unthinkable a generation earlier.

The party's more liberal attitude was reflected in drama, dance, music, and literature. In 1978 and 1979 alone, the newly established Foreign Literature Publishing House brought out more than seventeen million copies of classics of world literature. Homer, Dante, Shakespeare, Goethe, Dickens, and scores of other writers have been translated into Chinese. *World Literature,* a bimonthly journal, publishes contemporary American and European writing.

Chinese writing underwent remarkable changes in just a few years. New books and poems began to deal with love, romance, adventure, and even sex—subjects forbidden just a few years earlier. A "literature of the wounded" described the human suffering during the Cultural Revolution. More daring writers even hinted at problems in the underlying structure of socialist society.

The true extent of the new freedom for artists and writers in China is difficult to judge. Democracy Wall is a case in point. Democracy Wall stretches 200 yards (183 meters) along a boulevard leading to Tien An Men Square in Peking. In the late

Elaborately costumed members of a traditional Chinese opera company

1970s it served as a giant bulletin board for "big-character posters" expressing a wide variety of viewpoints on social and political affairs. An open letter to the editor of *Wenli Bao* (the Literary Gazette), posted in January, 1979, demanded that political censorship of writers be abolished. Yet in November of that year, a leading dissident writer was sentenced to fifteen years in prison for writing counter-revolutionary wall posters. The government announced new restrictions on freedom of speech, and by December, Democracy Wall was whitewashed. In 1983, Teng announced a crackdown on Western corruption in the arts and literature. Yet when President Reagan visited China in the spring of 1984, Democracy Wall was covered with posters advertising shiny new watches for sale.

In a society as changeable as China's there is always the danger of backlash against new forms of expression. The climate for artists seemed healthier in 1984 than at any other time since the founding of the People's Republic. But no one could tell how long the thaw would last.

MAP KEY

Acheng	B10
Aerhchin Mountains (Aitun Shan/Altyn Tagh)	D2,3,G11,12 (inset)
Aihui (Aigun)	B10,11
Ailan (Manas), lake	B2
Alashantsochi (Payenhaote)	D7
Altai (Altai/Sharasume)	B2
Altai mountains	B1,2,3
Anhwei (Anhui), province	E,F 9,10
Angangchi (Angangxi)	B9
Amur, river	A,B 8-10
Amne Machin, mountains	E6
Ankang	E7
Anking (Anqing)	E6
Apa	G4
Anshun	E6
Anyang	E7
Anlung (Anlong)	D7
Argun, river	G7
Brahmaputra (Yalutsangpu/Yarlung Zangbo), river	G8,9
Canton (Guangzhou)	F8,9
Chaling, lake	D8,9
Chalutechi (Jarud Qi)	B8
Chanchiang (Zhanjiang/Tsamkong)	G7
Chang (Yangtze), river	C,D 5,6,7,8
Changchih (Changzhi)	E8
Changchiakou (Zhangjiakou/Kalgan)	D8
Changchou (Hsinking)	C4
Changpei (Zhangbei)	C8
Changsha	F8
Changte (Changde)	F8
Changting	F9
Changtu (Chamdo/Qamdo)	E5
Changyeh (Zhangye)	D6
Chaoan (Zhaoan)	G9
Chaotung (Zhaotong)	F6
Chaoyang	C9
Chekiang (Zhejiang), province	E,F10
Chenchiang (Zhenjiang)	E9
Chengchou (Zhengzhou)	E8
Chenghai	F9
Chengku (Chenggu)	E7
Chengshan Chiao (Chengshan Jiao), point	D10
Chengte (Chengde/Jehol)	D9
Chengtu (Chengdu)	E6
Chenhsien (Chenzhou)	F8
Chenping	E7
Chenshih (Jianshui)	G6
Chiamussu (Jiamusi)	B11
Chinlin (Kirin)	C10

Chushan, region	B10
Dzungaria, region	B1,2,3
East China Sea	E,F 9,10
Ensihih	E7
Fanghsien (Fang Xian)	E7
Fengchien (Fengjie)	E7
Fengku (Fengdu)	E6
Fengtu (Fengdu)	G4
Fenyang	E8
Formosa Strait	F,G10
Fouhsin (Fuxin)	C9
Fouling (Fuling)	E7
Fouyang (Fuyang)	E8
Fuchin (Fujin)	B11,12 (inset)
Fuchou (Fuzhou/Foochow)	F9,10
Fuhai (Burjin Tokkol)	A,B2
Fuhsien (Dan Xian)	G8
Fulinchuan (Simao/Ssumao)	G6
Fukien (Fujian), province	F9,10
Funing	F9
Fushun	C9
Fuyu	B10
Gobi Desert	B,C 5,6,7,8
Grand Canal (Da Yunhe)	D,E 8-10,D,E6
Great Wall	F,G5
Greater Kingan Range (Da Hinggan Ling), mountains	A,B 8-10
Gulf of Chihli (Pohai/Bo Hai)	D9
Gulf of Tonkin	G7
Haichou (Guangzhou)	F3
Hailar (Hailaer/Hulun)	B7
Hailun	B9
Haikou (Hoihong)	G7
Hainan (Hainan), island	G,H 7,8
Haipowan	C7
Hami (Kumul)	C4
Hanchung (Hanzhong)	E7
Hangchou (Hangzhou)	E9,10
Han Shui, river	E,F 7,8
Hantan	E8
Harbin (Haerpin)	C10
Heiho (Nagchu)	C7
Heilungkiang (Heilongjiang), province	A,B 9-12
Hengshien (Heng Xian)	G7
Hengyang	F8
Himalaya, mountain range	F,G 2,3,4
Hofei (Hefei)	E9
Hohsien (He Xian)	F8
Holan Shan (Helan Shan), mountains	D7
Hong Kong (British)	G8
Honan (Henan), province	E8
Hopei (Hebei), province	D8
Hopu (Hepu)	G7
Hotien (Hotan)	D2
Hsi (West), river (Si Kiang/Xi Jiang)	G6,7,8
Hsiangtan (Xiangtan)	F8
Hsiapu (Xiapu)	F9
Hsichang (Xichang)	F5
Hsinchin (Xinjin/Pulantien)	D9
Hsingtai (Xintai)	E8
Hsinhsiang (Xinxiang)	E8
Hsinhui (Xinhui)	G8
Hsinmin (Xinmin)	C9
Hsinyang (Xinyang)	E8
Hsinyi (Xinyi)	G8
Hsuchang (Xuchang)	E8
Hsuchou (Suzhou/Suchow)	E8
Huai, river	E8,9
Huaiyang	B11
Huang Ho (Yellow), river	C,D 5,6,7,8
Huhsien (Hugu)	A9
Hunan (Hubei), province	E8
Ichang (Yichang)	E8
Ichun (Yichun)	B10
Ilan (Yilan)	B11
Inner Mongolia (Nei Monggol), autonomous region	C,D,E 5,6,7,8
Ipin (Yibin)	E6
Ishan (Yishan)	F6,7
Iyang (Yiyang)	F8
Kaerh (Gartok)	E2
Kaifeng	E8
Kaihsien (Gai Xian)	C9
Kanchou (Ganzhou)	F8

Kanchuerhmiao (Ganjur)	B8
Kangting (Kangding)	E5
Kansu (Gansu), province	D5
Kashih (Kashgar)	D1
Khanka, lake	B11
Kiangsi (Jiangxi), province	F8,9
Kirin (Jilin), province	C10
Kochiu (Gejiu)	G6
Koehmu	D4,5
Koko Nor (Tsingha/Qinghai), lake	D5
Kolamai (Karamai/Karamay)	B1
Korea Bay	D9
Koshan (Keshan)	B10
Kowloon (Hong Kong, British)	G8
Kuanghua	E7
Kuanghsien (Guanxian)	E6
Kueilin (Guilin)	F7
Kuehsien (Gui Xian)	G7
Kueiyang (Guiyang)	F6
Kuerlo (Korla)	C3
Kunlun Mountains (Kunlun Shan)	D2,3,4
Kunming	G6
Kwangsi Chuang (Guangxi), autonomous region	G7
Kwangtung (Guangdong), province	F,G 7,8
Kweichow (Guizhou), province	F6,7
Laichow Bay (Laizhou Wan)	D9
Lanchou (Lanzhou)	D6
Langchung (Langzhong)	E6
Lenghu	D4
Lesser Khingan Range (Xiao Hinggan Ling), mountains	B10
Lhasa (Lasa)	F3,H12 (inset)
Liaoning, province	C9
Liaotung Peninsula (Liaodong Bandao)	D9
Liaoyang	C9
Lichiang (Lijiang)	F5
Lienyunchiangshih (Lianyungang)	E9
Linfen	E8
Linchuan	F9
Linching (Linqing)	E8
Linhai	F10
Linhsia (Linxia)	D6
Lini (Linyi)	E9
Lintao	D6
Liping	F7
Lipu	F7,8
Lishui	F9
Liucheng	F7
Liuchou (Liuzhou)	F7
Loho (Luohe)	E8
Lop Nor, dry salt lake	C,D3
Loshan (Leshan)	E5
Loyang (Luoyang)	E8
Luan, river	D8,9
Luchou (Luzhou/Lusihen)	F6
Luhsien (Mei Xian)	F5
Luichow Peninsula (Leizhou Bandao)	G7,8
Lulung (Lulong)	D9
Lungchou (Longzhou)	G6
Lunglin (Longlin)	F6
Lushan	E8,9
Lushun (Port Arthur)	D9
Luta (Luda/Dairen)	D9
Macao (Macau), Portuguese Terr.	G8
Manassu Chuang (Manas), river	B2,C2,3
Manchuria, region	A,B,C 8,9,10,11
Maoming	G7
Maomu (Tinghsin)	B9
Meihsien (Mei Xian)	F8
Mekong (Lancang), river	G,7,8
Mengtzu (Mengzi)	G6
Mienning	F5
Min, river	F9
Mingshui	B10
Minya Konka (Gongga Shan), mountain	E5
Moho (Mohe)	A9
Mutanchiang (Mudanjiang)	C11
Namcha Barwa, mountain	F4
Namu (Nam Co/Tengri), lake	E3
Nan (Qilian Shan), mountains	D4,5,6
Nanchang	F8
Nanchung (Nanchong)	E6
Nanking (Nanjing)	E9
Nanning	G7
Nantung	E9,10
Nanyang	E7

Neichiang (Neijiang)	F6
Neihsiang (Neixiang)	E7
Ninghsien	F4
Ningpo (Ningbo)	F10
Ningsia (Ningxia), autonomous region	D7
Ningte (Ningde)	F9
Ningwu	D8
Nungan (Nang An)	C10
Ochina, river	C,D 4,5
Oling, lake	D4
Ordos Desert	D7
Paicheng	B9
Paise (Bose)	G6
Palikun (Barkol)	C3
Pamir, mountains	D1
Pangfou (Bengbu)	E8
Paocheng (Baocheng)	E6
Paochi (Baoji)	E7
Paoshan (Baoshan)	F5
Paoting (Baoding/Tsingyuan)	D8
Patan (Batang/Parr)	E4
Peian (Beian)	B10
Pehai (Beihai)	G6
Peking (Beijing)	D8
Penchih (Benxi)	C9
Pinghsiang (Pingxiang)	F8
Pichieh (Bijie)	F6
Pingle (Pingle)	F7
Pingtu (Pingdu)	D8
Pingwu	E6
Plateau of Tibet	E3,4,5
Ponsien (Bo Xian)	E8
Pokotu	B9
Poshan (Boshan)	D9
Poli (Boli)	B11
Possuteng Hu (Bosten Hu), lake	C2
Poyang, lake	F8,9
Puerh	G5
Putehachi (Yalu)	B9
Putien (Putian)	F9
Red, river	G5
Santai	E6
Shahsien	F9
Shanghai	E9,10
Shangchiu (Shangqiu)	E8
Shanhaikuan (Shanhaiguan)	D9
Shanshan (Pichan)	C3
Shansi (Shanxi), province	D7,8
Shantung (Shandong), province	D8,9
Shantung Peninsula (Shandong Bandao)	D9
Shaohsing (Shaoxing)	E9
Shaokuan (Shaoguan)	F8
Shaoyang	F7
Shashih	E8
Shashin	D6,7
Shensi (Shaanxi), province	E7
Shenyang (Mukden)	C9
Shihchiachuang (Shijiazhuang)	D8
Sian (Xian/Hsian)	E7
Sinkiang Uighur (Xinjiang), autonomous region	B,C 1,2,3
Soche (Shache/Yarkand)	D1
Solun (Solon)	B9
South China Sea	G,7,8
Ssuping (Siping)	C9,10
Ssunan (Sinan)	F7
Suchou (Suzhou)	E9
Suchuan (Chuguchak)	B1
Suifenho (Suifenhe)	C11
Suihsien (Sui Xian)	E7
Suihua	B10
Suite (Suide)	D7
Sungpan (Songpan)	E6
Swatow (Shantou)	F,G9
Szechwan (Sichuan), province	E5,6

Tangwang, river	B10
Tao (Tao'er), river	B9
Taotan	F7
Taohsien (Dao Xian)	F8
Tarim Darya, river	C2,3
Tatung	D8
Tayu (Dayu)	F8
Techin	F4
Techou (Dezhou)	D8
Teko	G6
Tepao (Debao)	G6
Tibet (Xizang, autonomous region)	E,F 2,3,4
Tiehling (Tieling)	C9
Tienpai (Dianbai)	G7
Tien Shan, mountains	C1,2,F10,11 (inset)
Tienshui (Tianshui)	E7
Tientsang	E9
Tientsin (Tianjin)	D8
Tinghai	E9
Tinghsien (Ding Xian)	D8
Tingli	E6
Tingnan (Dingnan)	F8
Tsaidam Basin	D3,4,5
Tsangchou (Cangzhou)	D8
Tsinan (Jinan/Chinan)	D8
Tsinghai (Qinghai), province	D4,5
Tsingtao (Qingdao/Chingtao)	D9
Tsunhua (Zunhua)	C8
Tsun (Zunyi)	F6
Tulufan (Turfan)	C2
Tunchi	E9
Tunghua (Tonghua)	C10
Tungkuan (Tongguan)	E7
Tungliao (Tongliao)	C9
Tungping (Dongping)	D8
Tungpu (Rangsum)	E4
Tungting (Dongting Hu), lake	F8
Tunhuang	C4
Turfan Depression	C2,3
Tushan (Dushan)	F6
Tuyun (Duyun)	F6
Tzukung	F6
Urumchi (Urumqi/Wulumachi)	C2,F11 (inset)
Ussuri, river	B11
Victoria (Hong Kong, British)	G7
Wanhsien (Wanxian)	E6,7
Wei, river	D,E7,8
Weichang	C8
Weifang	D8,9
Weihai	D9
Weihsi (Weixi)	F5
Weinan	E7
Wenchou (Wenzhou)	F9,G10
Wenshan	G6
Wu, river	F6,7
Wuchou (Wuzhou)	G7
Wuhan	E8
Wuhu	E9
Wuhsi (Wuxi)	E9
Wuhsing (Wuxing)	E9
Wukang	F7
Wulumku (Ulungur), river	B2
Wushan	E6
Wusu (Usu)	C1
Wutungchiao	G4
Wuyuan	C6
Yaan	B10
Yalung (Yalong), river	E,F5
Yangchiang (Yangjiang)	G7
Yangchuan	G6
Yangchun	D4
Yangtze (Chang), river	C,D 4,5,6,7,8
Yellow Sea	D9
Yellow (Huang Ho), river	C,D 5,6,7,8
Yenan (Yanan)	E6
Yenchi (Yanji)	C11
Yenchi (Yanqi/Karashahr)	E7
Yentai (Yantai/Chefoo)	D9
Yinchuan (Ningsia/Ningxia)	D7
Yinkou	C9
Yingte	G6
Yu (You), river	F,G7
Yuanchiang	G6
Yuanchuan	G7
Yuehyang (Yueyang)	C4
Yulin (Watlam)	D7
Yulin	F8
Yumen	F,G 11 (inset)
Yumenshih	D5
Yungan (Yangan)	F9
Yuncheng	E7
Yunhsien (Yun Xian)	E2,3
Yunnan, province	G5,6
Yunnan Plateau	G6
Yushu (Jyekundo)	E4

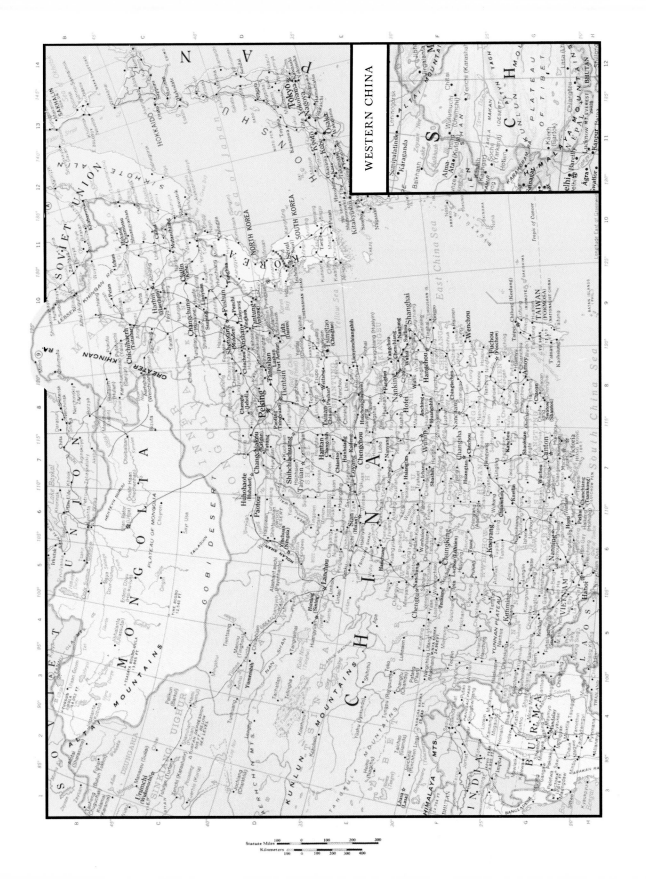

WESTERN CHINA

© Copyright by Rand McNally & Co., 84-S-18

Statute Miles
Kilometers

MINI-FACTS AT A GLANCE

GENERAL INFORMATION

Official Name: People's Republic of China (Chung-hua Jen-min Kung-ho-kuo/ Zhongguo Renmin Gongheguo)

Capital: Peking

Official Language: *Putonghua,* known as Mandarin in the West. Based on the northern Chinese dialect spoken in Peking, *putonghua* is taught in China's schools. Many minority languages are also spoken and taught in different parts of the country. These include Tibetan; Chuang; Miao and Yao; various Turkic languages, such as Uighur, Kazakh, and Khalkhas; Mongolian; Tungusic; and Korean.

Government: There are three major political organizations in Communist China—the Communist Party, the army, and the government. But the real power is the Chinese Communist Party. The party makes policy which the army and the government carry out. Local Communists elect representatives to one of twenty-nine Provincial Party Committees. These committees, in turn, send representatives to the National Party Congress, held about every five years. The National Party Congress elects a Central Committee of about two hundred members, who do the routine work of the party. The twenty-seven members of the Central Committee's Politburo (Political Bureau) are the most powerful group in China. The Politburo elects a Standing Committee and a Secretariat, which actually decide policy for the entire country. The chairman of the Standing Committee is the real head of the Chinese government. According to the 1979 constitution, the National People's Congress (not the same as the National Party Congress) is the only legislative authority in the country. In reality, its job is to rubber-stamp the decisions made by the Chinese Communist Party. Delegates to the National People's Congress are elected at the provincial level from a list drawn up by the party. On the advice of the party, the delegates appoint the members of the State Council, which oversees the government ministries and bureaus.

Flag: China's flag was adopted in 1949. In the upper left-hand corner, on a plain red background, is a large yellow star with a semicircle of four smaller yellow stars to its right. The stars stand for the Communist Party and its members.

Banners like this one urged citizens to cooperate in the 1982 census.

National Song: "March of the Volunteers"

Religion: After the Communist revolution, religious practice was discouraged and most churches and other places of worship were closed. By the early 1980s, however, the authorities were more lenient, allowing Buddhists, Muslims, Lama Buddhists, and Christians (who probably exceed the 1949 estimate of three to four million) to conduct religious services. The authorities also were permitting the training of clergymen and the publication of Bibles, hymnals, and other religious works. The estimate of the number of Muslims in China is anywhere from seven to more than ten million. The constitution guarantees religious freedom, but it also protects the "freedom not to believe" and to propagate atheism.

Money: The basic monetary unit in the People's Republic is the *Renminbi* (people's currency), or *yuan*. There are also the *fen* and the *jiao*. One *yuan* equals ten *jiao*. A *jiao* equals ten *fen*. There are 100 *fen* to a *yuan*. As of February, 1984, the rate of exchange was 2 *Renminbi (yuan)* to a U.S. dollar.

Weights and Measures: Most foreign trade is conducted in the metric system, but the Chinese have their own system for domestic activities. For example, the *jin (catty)* equals 1.102 pounds; the *dan (picul)* equals 0.0492 tons; and a *mu* equals 0.1647 acres.

Population: China's population was 1,031,882,511, including Taiwan, Hong Kong, and Macao, according to the 1982 census.

*Ch'eng-tu (Chengdu)
schoolchildren*

Cities:

Shanghai	11.8 million
Peking (Beijing)	9 million
Tientsin (Tianjin)	7.8 million
Chungking (Chongqing)	6 million
Ch'eng-tu (Chengdu)	3.6 million
Wuhan	3 million
Shenyang (Mukden)	2.5 million
Sian (Xian)	2.5 million
Nanking (Nanjing)	2.4 million
Canton (Guangzhou)	2 million
Haerh-pin (Harbin)	2 million
Lanchou (Lanzhou)	2 million

(These population statistics should be regarded as estimates.)

Dozens of bicycles are parked near a newspaper wall in Suchou.

Provinces	**Capital**
Anhwei (Anhui)	Hofei (Hefei)
Chekiang (Zhejiang)	Hangchou (Hangzhou)
Fukien (Fujian)	Fuchou (Fuzhou)
Heilungkiang (Heilongjiang)	Haerh-pin (Harbin)
Honan (Henan)	Chengchou (Zhengzhou)
Hopeh (Hebei)	Shih-chia-chuang (Shijiazhuang)
Hunan	Changsha
Hupeh (Hubei)	Wuhan
Kansu (Gansu)	Lanchou (Lanzhou)
Kiangsi (Jiangxi)	Nanchang
Kiangsu (Jiangsu)	Nanking (Nanjing)
Kirin (Jilin)	Changchun
Kwangtung (Guangdong)	Canton (Guangzhou)
Kweichow (Guizhou)	Kuei-yang (Guiyang)
Liaoning	Shenyang (Mukden)
Shansi (Shanxi)	Taiyuan
Shantung (Shandong)	Tsinan (Jinan)
Shensi (Shaanxi)	Sian (Xian)
Szechwan (Sichuan)	Ch'eng-tu (Chengdu)
Tsinghai (Qinghai)	Hsi-ning (Xining)
Yunnan	Kunming

Autonomous Regions	**Capital**
Inner Mongolia (Nei Monggol)	Hu-ho-hao-t'e (Huhetot/Hohhtot)
Kwangsi (Guangxi)	Nanning
Ningsia (Ningxia)	Yinchuan
Sinkiang (Xinjiang)	Urumchi (Ürümqi)
Tibet (Xizang)	Lhasa

GEOGRAPHY

Highest Point: Mount Everest (Chomolungma), 29,028 ft. (8,848 m)

Lowest Point: Turfan Depression, 505 ft. (154 m) below sea level

Coastline: 3,600 mi. (5,800 km) from the mouth of the Yalu River in the northeast to the Gulf of Tonkin in the south

Rivers: The longest river in China is the Yangtze River (Chang Jiang), 3,988 mi. (6,418 km); the second longest is the Yellow River (Huang Ho), 3,011 mi. (4,846 km).

Lakes: The largest salt lake in China is Tsinghai Lake (Kokonor) in Tsinghai (Qinghai) Province, 3,237 sq. mi. (8,384 km²).

Mountains: China is a mountainous country. It is estimated that regions 3,281 ft. (1,000 m) or higher above sea level comprise more than 68 percent of the total area of the country.

Climate: Because China is very large, its climate ranges from tropical to subarctic. But the difference in latitude is not the only factor influencing climate. There are also two others: altitude and distance from the sea. The city of Shanghai, on the coast, has an average January temperature of 38° F. (3.3° C) and an average July temperature of 80° F. (26.7° C). Urumchi (Ürümqi), located in the interior, has an average temperature in January of −3° F. (−19.4° C) and a July average of 75° F. (23.9° C). Rain in China falls mostly in the summer and much more on the southeast coast than other places. Parts of the interior have too little rain to support crops. There are large regions of deserts and steppes which are very desolate. The chief deserts are the Gobi, the Ordos, and the Takla Makan. Even in areas which are not deserts, the rainfall is unpredictable. Since the beginning of recorded history, China has been plagued by droughts and floods.

Greatest Distances: 2,500 mi. (4,023 km) from north to south; 3,000 mi. (4,828 km) from east to west

Area: 3,680,000 sq. mi. (9,530,000 km²)

NATURE

Trees: There are many kinds of trees in China. Oak, maple, linden, birch, Korean pine, walnut, and elm grow in the north. In the temperate climates, there are ginkgo and metasequoia. In the southern and southwestern provinces, 150 species of evergreen can be counted. Bamboo trees are found in large numbers south of the Yangtze. In the area bordering Korea, there are larch, spruce, and fir.

Animals: In the tundra—reindeer, arctic hare, arctic fox, wolf, and lemming. South of the tundra—brown bear, wolf, glutton, otter, ermine, sable, lynx, elk,

*Limestone hills line the Li River at Kueilin, thought
by many to be the most scenic spot in all of China.*

forest reindeer, hare, and several kinds of squirrel. In the mountains—takin, or
goat antelope. In and near Tibet—giant panda and wild yak.

Birds: In and around Tibet—pheasant and varieties of laughing thrushes. In the
tundra—willow grouse, ptarmigan, gray plover, sanderling, knot, and several
kinds of sandpiper. South of the tundra—black grouse, hazel hen, black
woodpecker, Siberian jay, and greater and lesser spotted woodpeckers.

Fish and other water animals: Shad, perch, bass, sturgeon, pike, loach, carp;
prawns, crabs, sea cucumbers, eels, herring, sharks; small species of alligator; giant
salamander.

EVERYDAY LIFE

Food: Grain is the staple of the Chinese diet. In most of China, this means rice,
although in northern China corn and wheat are very popular. The Chinese eat
many kinds of vegetables, but little meat. When they do eat meat, pork and poultry
are their favorites. Chinese cooking is popular throughout the world. To Western
palates, dishes such as shrimp dumplings or lotus soup are very exotic and
delicious. There are many types of Chinese food. Much Szechwanese food is spiced
with small red chilis. Cantonese food is sweeter and more colorful than food from

other regions. Canton is famous for its pastries—steamed dumplings stuffed with meat, sweet paste, or preserves; buns; and tarts of all varieties.

Homes: Housing in China for most of the population is very simple. Most urban workers live in two- or three-room houses or apartments. Two or more families share a kitchen and bath. Water often comes from a communal tap. Furnishings are simple. A family may own a bed for each member, a table and a few chairs, and perhaps a wardrobe or a few trunks. Under the responsibility system, increasing numbers of families began to acquire more possessions, including television sets and sewing machines. In poor rural areas, a home may be made of mud bricks and have packed-dirt floors. But people who live in more prosperous areas live in newer, two-story homes.

Holidays: (National)
January 1, New Year's Day
Spring Festival (Chinese New Year)
March 8, International Working Women's Day
May 1 (May Day), International Labor Day
August 1, People's Liberation Army Day
October 1, National Day

Culture: Mao Tse-tung's ideas on art and literature dominated the Chinese scene from the revolution until his death in 1976. He recognized the value of China's artistic heritage, but he also stressed the importance of politics in art. Chinese opera, for example, an art form with a seven-hundred-year history, was purged of bourgeois ideas. Under Mao, Chinese opera reflected the workers' struggle. In the art world, paintings idealizing tractor drivers and oil refineries replaced such traditional subjects as long-robed scholars and waterfalls. Artists generally supported the regime, and morale was high for the first seven years after the revolution. Hard times came for artists during the Hundred Flowers movement in 1957. Later, during the Cultural Revolution in the 1960s and early 1970s, Chiang Ch'ing and the other members of the Gang of Four conducted a bitter campaign against any art they disapproved of. After 1976, however, when the Gang of Four fell, a more liberal atmosphere was established. The traditional form of opera reappeared.

Sports and Recreation: Almost everyone in China engages in daily athletic activity, from the traditional Chinese *tai chi chuan* exercises to calisthenics or table tennis. Competition is played down and team playing is emphasized. The purpose of organized sports is to develop people "physically, morally, and intellectually." Even when athletes perform extraordinarily well, they say that their efforts were for the good of the party and the country.

Schools: China has made a great deal of progress in education since 1949. When the Communists took over, more than 80 percent of the population could neither read nor write. Some 94 percent of today's children receive a six-year primary school education. Fewer than half of these finish middle schools, college-preparatory institutes for children twelve to eighteen years old. Only about 2.3

percent of Chinese youth actually get to college. During the Cultural Revolution (1966-76), higher education suffered greatly. Many schools of higher education were shut down in an attempt to reform the system. Today, there are approximately 650 regular colleges and universities. Another approximately 170 institutions of the more unconventional variety, including short-term colleges and TV universities, are also open for higher education. Most of the ten thousand graduate students in 1981 were studying science and technology.

Health: As a result of advances in medical science and sanitation and the return to peacetime conditions, the health of the average Chinese citizen has vastly improved since the Communist revolution. The Chinese claim to have eliminated most major contagious diseases, with the exception of schistosomiasis, a blood disease caused by a parasite. Cancer and heart disease are considered to be major health problems. Other major causes of death are tuberculosis, malaria, typhus, hookworm, encephalitis, and amoebic dysentery. The Chinese practice a combination of modern Western medicine and their own traditional medicine, which includes the use of herbs and acupuncture. Acupuncture is a system in which needles are inserted into the body at specific points to alleviate pain or cure disease. "Barefoot doctors" are also used. Although they do not literally go barefoot, they are doctors who undergo intensive, but short, training programs in order to work in rural areas. They share the life of the peasant, and in addition to curing people of disease, they help prevent disease by checking drinking water, vaccinating people, and making sure that garbage is disposed of. Medical care is all but free in China. The people pay a very small amount each month for it.

ECONOMY AND INDUSTRY

Principal Products:
Agriculture: Soybeans, rice, wheat, millet, peanuts, tea, tobacco, cotton, corn, sorghum, barley, potatoes, sweet potatoes, sugarcane, fruit; hogs, sheep, goats
Mining: Coal, petroleum, iron ore, tungsten, antimony, tin, lead, manganese bauxite, zinc, uranium, salt
Manufacturing: Iron, steel, machinery, metalworking tools, textiles, motor vehicles, ships, locomotives, industrial chemicals
Chief Exports: Meat and fish, fruits and vegetables, tea and spices, crude oil, petroleum products, textile fibers, textile yarn, fabrics, rugs, clothing

Communication: For its size, China has relatively few radios, television sets, or telephones. There are 300 AM and 10 FM radio transmitters, 7 million television sets, and about 4.5 million telephones.

Transportation: There are 31,877 mi. (51,300 km) of railroads in China; 563,599 mi. (907,000 km) of highways; and 101,400 mi. (169,000 km) of inland waterways, 84,506 mi. (136,000 km) of which are navigable. There are 160 domestic air routes serving more than eighty cities. The People's Republic also has four international airports served by thirteen international carriers.

IMPORTANT DATES

About 50,000 B.C. — *Homo sapiens* (human beings) appear in China

About 2000 B.C. — Under the Hsia dynasty, towns and cities appear; writing develops

About 1500 B.C. — The Shang dynasty marks the real beginning of Chinese history

About 1100 B.C. — The Chou dynasty ushers in China's feudal age

About 500 B.C. — Chinese culture spreads south to the Yangtze River during the Warring States period; the teachings of Confucius and Taoism begin to take hold

221-206 B.C. — The unification of China under the Ch'in dynasty; Emperor Shih Huang-ti builds the Great Wall

202 B.C.-A.D. 221 — The Han dynasty doubles China's size; Confucianism declared the state philosophy

221-589 — During the Age of Disunity, Buddhism takes hold in China, alongside Confucianism and Taoism

589-907 — Under the Sui and T'ang, China becomes the world's largest country

907-960 — In the Five Dynasties period, warlords rule the south and barbarians capture the north

960-1280 — The Sung dynasty reunites the country; cities become the new tax base

1280-1368 — The Yuan (Mongol) dynasty relies on foreigners, including Marco Polo, to run the country

1368-1644 — The Ming dynasty restores native rule; European traders arrive

1644-1911 — Under the Ch'ing (Manchu) dynasty, wars with European powers and Japan put China under foreign control

1905 — Sun Yat-sen founds the Revolutionary League

1908 — P'u Yi crowned as last Manchu emperor

1912 — Republic of China ends the imperial system of government but fails to unite the country; Sun Yat-sen sworn in as first president of the republic; Yuan Shih-k'ai becomes second president of the republic

1917 — Russian Revolution

1921—Chinese Communist Party founded

1925—Sun Yat-sen dies; Chiang Kai-shek becomes leader of the Kuomintang

1927—Chiang Kai-shek sets up Nationalist government at Nanking

1931—Japan invades Manchuria

1934-35—Communists' Long March from south Kiangsi to Shensi Province, led by Mao Tse-tung, wins peasant support and develops future party leaders

1937-45—War with Japan

1946-49—Civil war between Nationalists and Communists

1949—Mao Tse-tung announces formation of the People's Republic of China; Chiang Kai-shek sets up Nationalist government (Republic of China) on Taiwan

1950—Communists occupy Tibet; Sino-Soviet Friendship Pact

1950-53—Korean War

1953—First Five-Year Plan announced

1956-57—Hundred Flowers movement

1958—Beginning of Great Leap Forward (second Five-Year Plan)

1959—Mao Tse-tung passes the job of chairman of the People's Republic to Liu Shao-ch'i, retains position of chairman of the Communist Party; China's split with the Soviet Union becomes public; Soviet Union withdraws financial and military aid

1962—Brief war with India; policy of "walking on two legs" initiated

1963—Russia signs limited nuclear test ban treaty with Great Britain and the United States

1964—China challenges Soviet Union for leadership of world communism; China explodes its first nuclear device

1966-69—Cultural Revolution throws many top leaders out of office, including Liu Shao-ch'i; schools and factories close; Chinese life is severely disrupted, especially in the cities

1969—Border clashes with Russia; U.S. President Richard Nixon lifts some travel and trade restrictions between China and the United States

1970—China launches its first satellite

1971—Table-tennis team from the United States invited to visit China; secret talks between Henry Kissinger and Premier Chou En-lai; China's seat on the Security Council at the United Nations is given to the People's Republic

1972—President Nixon visits China; Shanghai Communique issued; relations between China and the West improve

1976—Chou En-lai dies; major earthquake takes place near Peking; Mao Tse-tung dies; Premier Hua Kuo-feng replaces Mao as party chairman; Gang of Four arrested, including Mao's widow, Chiang Ch'ing

1977—Teng Hsiao-p'ing again rehabilitated, named vice-premier, vice-chairman of the party, and chief-of-staff of the People's Liberation Army

1978—Teng Hsiao-p'ing emerges as top leader of post-Mao China; new Ten-Year Plan calls for modernizing industry, agriculture, science, and defense

1979-80—United States and China normalize relations; Teng visits America; foreign trade increases by 30 percent; China's leaders emphasize slower growth, careful planning, more individual incentives; border war with Vietnam erupts in spring, 1980

1981—Chiang Ch'ing convicted of treason; Hua Kuo-feng resigns

1982—China approves new constitution; Teng appoints new defense minister (Chang Ai-p'ing) and foreign minister (Wu Hsueh-ch'ien); free-market economy expands; first communes reorganized to promote the responsibility system

1983—Teng launches campaign to rid the party of 3 to 5 million Maoists, or else reform them

1984—In January, Premier Chao Chi-yang visits the U.S. and holds "very warm" talks with President Ronald Reagan; Reagan visits China in the spring; Soviet delegation scheduled to visit in the fall; State Council decrees that all citizens over the age of sixteen are to be issued identity cards

IMPORTANT PEOPLE

Chang Ai-p'ing (Zhang Aiping) (1910-   ), defense minister, member of the State Council

Chang Ch'un-ch'iao (Zhang Chunqiao) (1914-   ), member of the Politburo, Central Committee of the Chinese Communist Party; member of the Gang of Four; arrested in 1976

Chao Chi-yang (Zhao Ziyang) (1919-   ), member of the Standing Committee of the Politbureau; minister of the State Commission for Restructuring the Economic System; premier, 1980-

Chiang Ch'ing (Jiang Qing) (1914-   ), wife of Mao Tse-tung, arrested in 1976 as member of the Gang of Four

Chiang Kai-shek (1887-1975), president of the Republic of China, Taiwan

Chou En-lai (Zhou Enlai) (1898-1976), Chinese Communist leader and first premier of the People's Republic

Chu Teh (Zhu De) (1886-1976), marshal, commander in chief, Chinese Red Army, 1931-54; organized Long March in 1934 with Mao Tse-tung

Confucius (551-479 B.C.), one of China's greatest teachers, author of a code of behavior which lasted until the twentieth century

Dalai Lama of Tibet (1935-   ), Buddhist religious leader and former ruler of Tibet

Hu Yao-pang (Hu Yaobang) (1915-   ), Communist Party chairman, 1981; general secretary of the Communist Party

Hua Kuo-feng (Hua Guofeng) (1921-   ), Communist Party chairman, 1976-1981

Kublai Khan (1216-1294), founder of the Mongol dynasty

Lin Piao (Lin Biao) (1907-1971), Chinese Communist general, designated Mao's successor in 1969

Liu Shao-ch'i (Liu Shaoqi) (1898-1974), chairman of the republic, 1959-69; out of favor during Cultural Revolution

Lu Hsün (Lu Xun) (1881-1936), pseudonym of Chou Shu-jen, author of short stories and in later years Communist revolutionary writings

Mao Tse-tung (Mao Zedong) (1893-1976), leader of the Chinese Communist Party and founder of the People's Republic

P'u Yi (Pu Yi) (1906-1967), last Manchu emperor, also known as Hsuan-T'ung, K'ang-te, and Henry P'u-i

Shih Huang-ti (259-209 B.C.), emperor, first ruler to unify China

Sun Yat-sen (1866-1925), founder of the Revolutionary League and founding father of the Republic of China

Teng Hsiao-p'ing (Deng Xiaoping) (1904-   ), chairman of the Chinese Communist Party's Advisory Commission and Military Commission

Wu Hsüeh-ch'ien (Wu Xueqian) (1921-   ), member of the State Council; foreign minister, 1982-

Yü (circa 2000 B.C.), emperor, semilegendary founder of the Hsia dynasty

Yuan Shih-k'ai (Yuan Shikai) (1859-1916), general of the imperial army during the 1911 revolution and later president of the republic

Yung Lo (1360-1424), Ming emperor, 1403-24

INDEX

Page numbers that appear in boldface type indicate illustrations

About the Author

Valjean McLenighan, a graduate of Knox College in Galesburg, Illinois, became interested in writing children's books during her stint as an editor at a large midwestern publishing company. Since that time, many of her children's books have been published.

Though she nearly always has a book project in the works, Valjean finds time for a variety of other interests including the theater, children's television, and travel. She lives on the North Side of Chicago.